A Dry And Thirsty Land

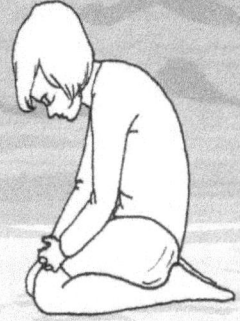

Making It Through Tough Times

By
Marilyn Marinelli

Copyright

Copyright: 2005 by Marilyn Marinelli, PO Box 831413, Ocala FL. 34483. All rights reserved. Printed in the United States of America. No part, portion or excerpt may be used, in any form, without the written permission of the author.

ISBN: 978-1-0878-7188-2

Table of Contents

About The Author v
Introduction vi
Chapter 1 How Long Oh Lord? 1
Chapter 2 Rejoicing In God's Love 4
Chapter 3 Are You Thankful? 9
Chapter 4 New Beginnings 14
Chapter 5 What Happened To Your Once Upon A Time? 18
Chapter 6 Resurrection Power Working In Your Life 22
Chapter 7 A Dry And Thirsty Land 25
Chapter 8 My Soul Longs For Thee 28
Chapter 9 Child of God, Why Do You Fear? 32
Chapter 10 When Nobody Cares, God Is There 34
Chapter 11 The Flesh & The Spirit 36
Chapter 12 Mattress or Faith 39
Chapter 13 Miracles Still Happen 44
Chapter 14 Lost But Not Forgotten 48
Chapter 15 Close The Doors And Walk On 50
Chapter 16 To Share In His Love 54
Chapter 17 Dealing With A Critical Spirit 57
Chapter 18 Don't Let Others Keep You Bound ... 60
Chapter 19 Godly Counsel 64
Chapter 20 God Is Still Speaking, " Are You Still Listening?" 67
Chapter 21 You Can Still Be A Blessing 71

Chapter 22	Are You Walking In Faith or Under The Law?	74
Chapter 23	Hope In The Midst of Change	80
Chapter 24	Restoring Your Peace	84
Chapter 25	In The Fullness of Time	90
Chapter 26	Word From The Lord To Us All	92
Chapter 27	It's Time To Move On	96
Conclusion		98
A Final Thought		102

About The Author

Marilyn Marinelli

Marilyn Marinelli is and Ordained Minister of the gospel associated with Faith Christian Fellowship Int'l, a worldwide full gospel fellowship. She is also the Co-Founder of the Fellowship of Christian Poets, a worldwide ministry, and Co-author of "Together Forever" a marital enrichment seminar.

She was a contributing author, poet and playright for the Fellowship of Christian Poets for over ten years. She hosted a monthly article called "Ministry to the Poets Soul".

Marilyn is also the founder and President of Have A Heart for Companion Animals, an information and referral website for the rescue, care and education of companion animals. (www.haveaheart.us) No More Homeless Pets.

One of her deepest desires is to share the knowledge of God, with others that have lost their hope. Her greatest joy is to stand on the Word of God, and see people being set free from bondage through her ministry.

She is inspired by the Holy Ghost, and often receives revelations from God in many situations.

All the Glory goes to God for His mercy and grace that He has shared with her and is still sharing in times of need.

Introduction

"A Dry And Thirsty Land" is a collection of specific teachings related to going through the dry and thirsty land of the soul. It is reflective of those times in which we all experience loneliness, heartache and yes, even despair. Psalm 63:1 "O God, thou art my God; early will I seek thee: my soul thirsteth for thee, my flesh longeth for thee in a dry and thirsty land, where no water is."

It is my hope that all who read this book will be blessed by the "how to get through" approach and faith that is presented in each chapter.

My hope, in compiling the subject matter for this book, is to share the truth that God never left me alone, not even in my darkest time. Instead, He encouraged me to go on and make it through.

We all want to believe a darkened, time will not come our way but, when it does, it helps to know that God will never leave us or forsake us in our time of need.

We can not see through the clouds of our life at all times but if we can remember that when there is only one beam of light leading to God, we can rest assure that the clouds will pass, the waves will stop overflowing our souls and the sunshine will arise in our hearts.

May God bless you as you read "A Dry And Thirsty Land". Be encouraged that your nights can turn into days of joy and peace, if only you trust and stand on God's word.

CHAPTER 1

How Long Oh Lord?

How long oh Lord, do I search for you in the midst of my feelings of sadness? Are you sitting in a season of time when your days roll into nights, and nights into days? When the difficulties of life keep rolling in like waves of the sea? Do you find yourself saying, "Where are you my Lord, my Savior? Why does this darkness cover my soul as a blanket day and night?"

Yes, I have been there. You are not alone. I'd like to share with you how the Lord helped me to walk out of that time.

I was sitting in the waves of sorrow that were rolling in towards me. I went to my husband and he shared with me what he could from the Lord. My husband, basically said, "When you turn it over to the Lord, this time of darkness will end." Well, that's just great, I thought. I could try, but the waves of sadness hit so strong, knocking me from side to side. I didn't even have the ability to think faith. It was as if a person was swimming and the waves kept hitting and hitting. After awhile the shoreline was not in clear sight.

God has His ways to help us. I purchased a cassette by Kenneth Copeland. The tape was full of songs that I hoped would bring me into a state of worship. All of a sudden, as I was listening to the tape, a song came on which confirmed what my husband had shared with me previously and further encouraged me to reach out to the Lord.

The special words in this particular song were "**how will it end, look to Him**". I played this song over and over to get it into my soul ... sometimes very loud to close out the voices urging me on to wallow in the unhappiness I was feeling.

Jesus said "I will never leave you or forsake you" God says, "See I have engraved you in the palm of my hand".

As I sat in my car, with the rain pouring down on my windshield, and tears streaming down my face, God spoke to me and said "The raindrops on your window are my angels crying for you today". I said, "Oh, God, you have more to say to me, don't you?" I grabbed a pen and some paper of sorts from my purse and proceeded to pen what God spoke to my heart that day:

Teardrops From Heaven

The teardrops on your window
Are the teardrops from my angels
Crying for you ...

To let you know you are not alone.
My tears fill your broken heart
And comfort you in this time of need.

They are tears from heaven
That flow from my throne
To let you know
That you are not alone.

For when you are saddened
My heart cries for you,
To send comfort to you.

Teardrops from heaven
For you this day
Streaks your window
Reflecting your inner cry of sadness.

My comfort to you this day
Are teardrops on your windshield.
Tears from heaven
To help wash away the sorrow.

Teardrops from heaven.
Teardrops as I cry for you
To let you know I am close
To healing your pain.

Teardrops from heaven
Teardrops from heaven.

By: Marilyn Marinelli

Herein, began the healing of my soul. The waves became less strong and the faith and love of God started to grow stronger. I remembered Psalm 23 "The Lord is my Shepherd. The Lord is my Shepherd"... sometimes God will only give us a little bit of His word to strengthen us. Remember, "The Lord is my (your) Shepherd" too.

CHAPTER 2
Rejoicing In God's Love

I have a great story to tell you. Now you have to understand that I am not a perfect Christian. Are you? If you are, you should think again, for no one is perfect, but Jesus.

Anyway, I have had a very hard time over the past year. I lived in sadness most of the time, struggling with my walk with God, because of the enemy's attack. It was as if every time I got up, I was spun around and punched. Men could relate to this, when I say it was like being in a boxing match, when things really get heated.

God is so good to us, when we don't give up. I felt I was hanging on with a thread somehow attached to God. Many things were attacking my walk with God, so that I would give up on following Him. But, in my deep despair I still called out to God for help and he answered my call.

I had to do some things, like make an effort to seek Him and His Word, yet I couldn't read my bible. I didn't want to sing praises. I didn't want to hear preaching and I didn't want to be around any Christians. That is how deep my despair was. Yet deep inside, I didn't want to walk away from God. Waves of darkness consumed my soul. And fear tried to take hold. When I went to church, a song or a word of preaching spun me into tears of sadness. Needless to say, I was afraid to go to church, because I didn't want to cry any more.

What about my husband? Of course, he tried to share God's wisdom with me. I heard but couldn't apply things and I understood yet, the pull on me became stronger. Mind you, I didn't want to run from God, but I guess I was running away from circumstance and thereby, I also found myself running away from God.

I realized finally, that I had a choice to make. There are always two roads to walk. You walk with God or walk away from Him. After all the blessings I received and the times God has used me to minister to others, I really didn't want to give up my walk with Him.

But sometimes, I am sorry to say, there are people around us that are Christians and yet are not really walking in God's love and wisdom, yet they think they are. These people can really trip you up. I urge you to watch out for them. Keep your walk with God and **Stay in His Word**.

Regardless of the circumstances, I tried to listen to Christian music and was blessed from time to time. Then I started to listen to TBN and God started speaking to me through Jan Crouch and her story of depression (great testimony), Kenneth Copeland, Creflo Dollar, Joyce Myers and a minister from Ft. Lauderdale, all of them unbelievably, preached on the same subject …Get Out of the Boat and walk on the water to Jesus. Just reach out and Jesus will be there for you.

Finally, God's message got through to me and this is what happened. I pray I can express it all properly to you.

I had just listened to pastor Dollar preaching and said, "OK God, I am going in my room and get things in order with you." So I went in my room, took off my shoes and in my heart said, "God I'm coming to you and taking my shoes off like Moses did, so I can walk on Holy Ground." No sooner did I sit down on my bed and put my bible in front of me and prayed, "God I understand your message. I want to come back to you," then I heard a faint cry of a cat (meow) and thought oh, another lost animal. I have to stop for a minute and tell you, not only through my time of sadness did I come across a lot of sad women, but also have helped rescue a few dogs and a cat. Almost every other week, when I would go out, I would see a lost dog... at least 5 in the past month. We don't live in the wilderness. There are many homes here so where were they coming from? There are so many lost people and animals.

To go on with what happened, I started to speak to God again, but I heard another cry of a cat (meow, meow). "Oh it's my cat. He must be shut up in the closet by accident." Sure enough, it was my cat Sammy that I heard crying, and of course, I rescued him from his dilemma.

My two dogs came running in and jumped on the bed to see what was happening. They were rejoicing with me and began kissing Sammy, my cat too. Why am I telling you this story? Where does God fit into this? Well, let me tell you the most remarkable thing.

The preacher I was listening to said, "Jesus has His hand reaching out to you. All you have to do is reach back and you can walk on the water with Him and get out of the storm."

God revealed to me that since I reached out to Him with understanding and made an effort to follow Him, He was already there for me and was rejoicing that I had come back home to Him. Now let me tell you the funniest thing. God has a sense of humor and also uses things we can understand to understand Him.

While I was rejoicing on getting Sammy, my cat, out of the darkness of the closet, God was showing me in my spirit how He was rejoicing over me, that I chose to reach out to Him and He was taking me out of my closet of darkness. God's word from the bible to me at that time was, Luke 19:10 "For the Son of man came to seek and to save that which was lost."

My two dogs, God showed me, were rejoicing and wondering what was going on and kissing Sammy, my cat, was a picture of God's angels rejoicing with Him …that I had come back home to God. I laughed and laughed and laughed, how God could use this circumstance to show me His joy and now I found myself rejoicing and laughing with God. Not only did God show me all this joy but He also allowed me a little of how much joy He had over me on my return. He did this every time I touched Sammy. A tremendous amount of joy would flow through me and God kept saying to my spirit, **"This is joy I feel for you"**. Every time I touched my dogs, God allowed me to feel some of what He feels when He touches His Angels. God and me, laughed for the longest of time and joy returned back to my soul (mind, will and emotions).

The next thing that happened was, that my dogs and I went out in the backyard and they ran and ran and ran with lots of life streaming in abundance. And as I rejoiced in the backyard, thanking God, He spoke to my spirit again and said, **"Life streams from Me. There is an abundance of life in My world."**

II Corinthians 3:5 says…"Not that we are sufficient of ourselves to think of anything as being of ourselves, but our sufficiency is from God." And Psalms 66:5 says, "Come and see the works of God: He is awesome in His doing toward the sons of men."

MARILYN MARINELLI

The last scripture the Lord shared with me was Psalms 16:7..."
Return to your rest oh my soul for the Lord has dealt bountifully
with you."

CHAPTER 3
Are You Thankful?

Are you thankful for what God has done for you? Have you been seeking His direction, your own or someone else's?

Faith Is the Substance

I would like to share a teaching that the Lord gave me on Faith. Faith is the substance of things hoped for. Now, realize that you can have faith in the good things of God or faith in bad things that are not of God. The word, "substance" means – standing under the claim. The claim to the property supports its validity. Thus, faith is a title deed, your right to have and use. You may have hope, but you have nothing of substance to stand on: use faith. It is your substance.

Here's a question for you: How can you have faith if you don't hear God's Word or read His Word? As we know, "Faith comes by hearing and hearing from the Word of God". Look to God for a revelation from His Word to you, and then stand on it.

Let's look at a few scriptures, these will show us that it wasn't the faith that Jesus had that healed someone, but the faith the person had that reached out to Him that healed them. It's like a plug and a socket. Put them together and you get a flow of electricity. Your faith in Jesus and the faith that is in Him couples together and you have a divine flow.

MARILYN MARINELLI

Matthew 9:29 "Then touched he (Jesus) their eyes saying, According to your faith, be it unto you." Matthew 9:22 "But Jesus turned him about and when he saw her, he said, "**Daughter, be of good comfort; thy faith has made thee whole.**" Matthew 8:10 "When Jesus heard it, he marveled, and said to them that followed, Verily I say unto you, I have not found so great faith, no, not in Israel." (with anyone)

Matthew 9:2 "Behold, they brought to him a man sick of the palsy, lying on a bed: and Jesus, seeing their faith said unto the sick of the palsy; Son, be of good cheer; thy sins be forgiven thee." Let's see what is in your title deed, as I mentioned above. Take a look at Hebrews. This is where the Lord showed me how to walk in faith.

Hebrews 11:3 "Through faith we understand that the worlds were framed by the Word of God, so that **things which are seen were not made of things which do appear.**"

Hebrews 11:4 – Shows us that we need to offer obedience and sacrifice to God.

Hebrews 11:5 - Please God – How? By taking God at His word.

Hebrews 11:6 - Seek God diligently, and believe He is a rewarder of them that diligently seek him.

How can you walk in faith? God showed me by reading through Hebrews 11.

If we look at the following, we will see a flow and application for walking in faith.

HEBREWS 11:7 – "By faith Noah, being warned of God of things not seen as yet, moved with fear" Notice Noah was TOLD of God.

HEBREWS 11:8 – Abraham by faith was called of God to go out into a place and he OBEYED, not knowing where he went. – You OBEY God's direction

HEBREWS 11:9 – "By faith he (Abraham) sojourned in the land of promise." Abraham made a move. MOVE in your circumstance based on what God tells you.

HEBREWS 11:11 – "Through faith also Sara herself RECEIVED strength to conceive seed" Your part is to RECEIVE by faith what God shows you.

HEBREWS 11:17 – "By faith Abraham, when he was tried, offered up Isaac; and he that had received the promises offered up his only begotten."

Your part is to LAY DOWN YOUR CIRCUMSTANCE TO GOD, FOR HIM TO RAISE UP. You leave it in God's hands. What else do you do?

When I read HEBREWS 11:20-25, I saw that I would be blessed. I should be thankful and sing praise and worship to God. I should also depart from the situation, not sit in fear and refuse to accept the circumstance or situation. I need then, to remember that I left the care in God's hands to work out.

As I read further in Hebrews 11:26-31 this is what was revealed to me:

1. I should hold up the riches, blessings of God higher than the benefits of what others can give me or sin can give to me.

2. I should leave the situation and don't fear but trust God.

3. I should keep my walk with God and pass through or move over to the New Life in my situation.

4. I will then see the walls fall down concerning this problem and everlasting life will be shed in that situation.

These are the 11 RULES OF FAITH that God shared with me.

1. YOU ARE TOLD OF GOD
2. YOU OBEY GOD
3. YOU MOVE IN GOD
4. YOU RECEIVE OF GOD
5. YOU WALK IN THE BLESSING
6. YOU WORSHIP GOD
7. YOU LEAVE SIN
8. YOU LEAVE THE PLACE OR SITUATION
9. YOU WALK IN NEW LIFE (pass thru)
10. YOU SEE OLD WALLS FALL DOWN
11. YOU HAVE EVERLASTING LIFE IN THE SITUATION (victory)

The last two things I want to share with you are the last two scriptures that were given to me, as I sought the Lord that day.

I Peter 3:12 "For the eyes of the Lord are over the righteous, and his ears are open unto their prayers: but the face of the Lord is against them that do evil."

I Peter 2:9 "But ye are a chosen generation, a royal priesthood, an holy nation, a peculiar people; that ye should show forth the praises of him who hath called you out of darkness into his marvelous light." Called chosen, called to show forth praises in every situation.

I pray you have been blessed, encouraged not to give up and that you gain many victories by standing on God's Word that are His promise's, just for you.

CHAPTER 4
New Beginnings

NEW BEGINNINGS ... The trees have lost their leaves only to stay dormant for a while. New beginnings will soon start. New leaves, deep in the tree's heart, will start to show and by summer the new leaves will be on the trees to bless us once again.

Have you been feeling that way lately? Have you felt you were losing leaves as though parts of your life were falling to the ground? I was.

God's Word tells us that there is a time for each season, and so it is in our own lives.

Things and people, we never wanted to leave, have passed from our sight. Only through God's love, grace and mercy can we find new beginnings. I have found this to be so.

My prayer for you is that you would look forward to the new things God has for you. Deep within your heart, new beginnings will start to be birthed. Can't you feel it? Don't you know God loves you? He said, "I will never leave you or forsake you."

God has you in the palm of His hand. Sometimes we are so overwhelmed with fears, doubts and concerns, from day to day that they can overwhelm us and keep us in the flesh. But, wait stop! Don't you know that we need to walk in the Spirit and not in the flesh? God wants us to be blessed. He knows our every tear and every hurt. Can't you see He is the one that is there?

So what if we put on some weight by eating too much until our tummies aches. There is always a new beginning with God. He says He will direct our paths. God is a lamp unto our feet. He is our Shepherd.

So what if the car broke down. Didn't God say He will supply all our needs? God can give you a fresh love to share. God can take away your every care.

So let's stop all the fuss. Kiss your wife or husband, or kiss the face of God and let's get to praying and seeking God first. Didn't He say in His Word, "Seek ye first the kingdom of God and all these other things shall be added unto you." If you don't seek God first, how can anything else fall into place?

I don't know about you but as for me, I'm thanking the Lord everyday for restoring me.

You know, I'm looking for His hand in my life. Those new leaves that are beginning to form that will shape my springtime and summer, so that I can go on and be beautiful in His sight and to others that pass my way. What about you?

I come from the Bronx, New York…so in my way of speaking, I would put it this way,

"Do you have enough nerve to trust God? Do you have the guts to go on and let God make a difference in your life?

So, stop sitting around and feeling all sad inside and saying, "I can't do it." Of course not, but with God, All Things Are Possible. Just seek His direction and stick to it. There are others just waiting for you. There are husbands waiting for that hug or wives waiting for that touch. Children longing for you to smile, puppy dogs and kitty cats needing your attention and if you are single, so what? Seek God. He will provide for you in all that you do. If you put Him first, you will be able to feel the love of God just for you. "

So what do you say, my Christian friends? Let's go on and be the best we can be. Let's pick ourselves up, dust ourselves off, and go on with God and. **Shine….Shine….Shine**

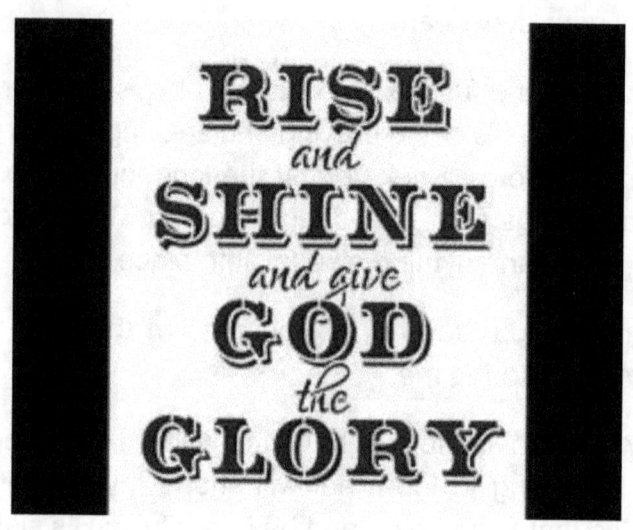

I AM

The sadness that lingers within your soul,
Is musty & covered with hurts of old.
Time passes each day & fear & loneliness fills your mind.
Thoughts of sadness from unforgotten times.

Your dreariness of mind will be stopped of its strain.
Cannot you see I removed all the care?
Don't you know I'm with you when loneliness is there?

All you must do through this time of despair,
Is to know my friend, "I AM" is there.
"I AM" your tomorrows "I AM" all your peace.
"I AM" all your joy, "I AM" sweat release.

A DRY AND THIRSTY LAND

All your tomorrows will cover this fear.
Your sadness & sorrow will never be near.
The stress & the strain that has kept you bound,
Will be released & never be found.

Your tomorrows will fill a cup in time,
Of memories lost of a forgotten time.
So do not fear or fret, my child, my salvation draws near
For in this loss of time, my love will adhere.

I hear you in your dark despair.
There is never a time that "I AM" is not there.
For in your darkness, doubts & fears,
A new creature, I make you, throughout all your tears.

The times are past. A new light will shine,
Through your weary sadness of heart & broken time.

I repair all the worry & fear & frets.
For "I AM" your Savior. There will be no regrets.

A time of renewing like fresh falling rain.
Will cause you to grow & remove all the strain.
A new heart I'll give you. A new walk in time,
Filled with my blessings, you'll always be mine.

I'll give you new tomorrows that will shine as a light.
Everything will be better. I'll make things all right.
No more will you wander on roads of despair,
For I have overcome this time of care.

So don't forget who is holding your hand,
"I AM" is with you as you walk thru this land.
"I AM" all your tomorrows, "I AM" all your peace,
"I AM" all your strength, "I AM" your sweet release.

Written By
Marilyn Marinelli

CHAPTER 5

What Happened To Your Once Upon A Time?

Where do you go when there is an end to all you had dreamed? When your thoughts differ from your spouse causing you not to be able to walk on together as one? A silence, a struggle to go on and make things interesting and exciting as it once was. What happened to our " Once Upon A Time", with all its hopes, dreams and desires?

All the times of trying and then we just give up? Did the strain of things just put us so far down that we can't seem to get up? When did the desire to achieve leave? When did our hearts fear? When did our desire to go on stop? When did too many situations leave us feeling that we couldn't make it anymore? How and why does it seem so hard to go on and fill our days with joy, wonder and excitement? **How did we lose our "Once Upon A Time?"** How did we lose our desire for life? Why was it stolen, or why did we let it go?

The struggles of everyday existence seem to zap our energy. Why? How come? Why does each day seem like a void to fill? Why does it seem that no matter how much we try, our lives seem empty. So much so that T.V. seems to be the only refuge.

Is it a fear of failure? Is that it? We try only to fail again? Does it mean that every time we try, we should win? Or does it mean we get up and go on with it, laughing at the failures and going on to better things and remembering the victories and the great fun in trying. How about just the joy of doing and the people we have touched along the way. Doesn't any of that count?

To try and fail; to try and fail; Anger, Hostility, A Void…A Lack of Care, A Lack of Concern, Boredom, Sorrow, Unfeeling.

The kids are grown… so that's it? They didn't fulfill our dreams of family? Whose kids really do? Alone together, we drift, looking and searching for a dream. When will it be there for us? Probably never, so if not, does that mean that our life stops? **Nooooooo!**

It means only that failure has tried to rear its ugly head. But whose failure is it? Not mine. Not yours. **It's the fear of failure that keeps us down.**

Jobs have lost their meaning. Bosses are unfeeling and uncaring. **Soooooo?** Money flows from God, not them. Our well-being and adjustments do not come from jobs, bosses, children or family. Our well-being comes from God in whom we move and live and have our being.

Immediately, the tide of life begins to ebb and flow, starting a stream trickling within ones soul. The things so important to each of us, do not measure up, but God knew that from the beginning. He knew who would be there for us. Questions upon questions;

Why do we spend our days in the, "why's of life", sitting and wondering why?????

Who cares anyway? Doesn't it mean we are to go on with hope in God? Doesn't it say in the Bible "Hope thou in God"? It never said, hope thou in other people. God gives us our dreams, our desires and divine appointments with others. So why stay trapped in the yesterdays that didn't pan out? Why suffer in the dreams that fell apart? Why not seek strength in God? Why not enjoy life and make new commitments to one another and stick to them? Why think on the past?

Why care about yesterday? Why not make new memories and have a zest for life? There is plenty of sadness. Look around… better yet, don't look around. Look to God, for He says to think on good things. Things of good report. God says in the Bible that He wants us to have life and to have it more abundantly. (John 10:10) So, what do you say? Do we dream more dreams? Do we make a commitment to go on and accomplish, pursue, pull ourselves up and be winners? Or do we just sit back and let the yesterdays crush our spirit?

I say go for it. Go for everything…. for your heart's desire…and dress the part. Don't let the expectations of others dictate how you dress. Dress for you; dress for your spouse; dress for your cause.

Get up! Stand up! Stand therefore; in Christ… in the anointing He has given you. Stand fast and don't be entangled in the yoke of bondage that leads to fear. Fear is not of God, but faith is, faith for what? For your dreams, sitting in a pile waiting for you to pick them up; for lost desires that have been buried under fear.

What do you do with dirty clothes? You wash them. Wash the fear out of your dreams and desires that God has given you. Don't use Tide…rather use the Word of God. Wash those fears away and let your dreams and desires sparkle. Don't put them in a dryer to dry. Hang them on the line so all that pass by can see who you are. Think about it; not everyone that passes by takes time to look at your clothes drying on the line. But you know they are there, clean and ready for someone to wear them. So will your dreams and desires be there for others who take the time to see them and be blessed?

I lost my dreams. They became like dirty clothes. They began to get gray and very old. The dreams I had, used to shine, but now, they don't. It seems like I'm carrying a load. Too much time has past, you see; there is nothing left for me. But wait just a minute, can this really be? God hasn't stopped helping me. He set me free... Free from the toil of a dreary day free to be me, even if you go away. Now, I have my dreams. God has given them to me. So if I fail or become a success, I know that I have tried.

Here's what the Lord told me:

"My dreams are your tomorrows. They are hidden in time. They are there if you want them to be. They are measured like the sands of the sea."

CHAPTER 6
Resurrection Power Working In Your Life

When spring passes, summer comes and the light of God shines in your darkness.

Micah 7:7 " I will look unto the Lord; I will wait for the God of my salvation: my God will hear me."

This, to me, is a statement that brings "Resurrection Power" into my life. The following scripture in Micah says something very powerful that helps me as I wait upon the Lord.

Micah 7:8 "Rejoice not against me, O mine enemy: when I fall, I shall arise; when I sit in darkness, the Lord shall be a light unto me."

Luke 9:56 says, "For the Son of man is not come to destroy men's lives, but to save them."

Where are you? Is your light shining? Are you living in a resurrected life? Or has the light grown dim?

Remember that Jesus came to give us life and to give it to us more abundantly. Are we missing that abundance by putting our energies into the wrong things? Do we miss the very blessings God has given us by running here and there and not focusing on the true blessings of God for our life, that are right in front of us everyday?

God seems to place, what we think are simple things or obvious circumstances right in front of us and yet we stumble over them trying to get to something else we think will bring us an abundant life.

Here are simple or obvious things like: Sunsets, stars in the sky, husbands, wives, children, pets, kind words, etc. I think you get the picture.

How about your enemies? Who are they? The people that steal your time away from the very blessings God has given you to enjoy. The uncaring people that trample the words God has spoken to your heart. These are just a few examples.

Sit and be quiet before the Lord. Again, who or what are your enemies? Who is taking time away from you, and your abundant life of love that God has given you? Haven't you wasted enough time running to and fro and never really been able to reap the benefits of God's blessing for you? If you agree, you're losing the resurrection power in this area of your life.

Don't let others steal your joy or peace. Allow God to resurrect your relationships with those He has placed in your life.

Stay in the Word, apply God's truths, be blessed and strengthened in Him. Others will then say what a terrific life you are having and ask, "How do you do it?" and you will be able to tell them, "Resurrection Power" has been at work in me.

Zephaniah 3:17 "The Lord thy God in the midst of thee is might; he will save, he will rejoice over thee with joy; he will rest in his love, he will joy over thee with singing."

MARILYN MARINELLI

Mark 10:52 "Go thy way; thy faith hath made thee whole."

As I Was On The Cross

I saw you as I was on the cross,
Your sadness and your pain.
I knew you needed hope,
That your life was filled with shame.

I knew you would be weary,
And would lose all hope to fear.
But, my child, I tell you
My salvation will adhere.

For every sorrow, pain and fear,
And for every doubtful thought,
I died for you that day,
Your salvation, I have bought.

Written By
Marilyn Marinelli

CHAPTER 7

A Dry And Thirsty Land

A dry and thirsty land, parched with no water, cracking, split and broken. Job 42:10 "And the Lord turned the captivity of Job, when he prayed for his friends: also the Lord gave Job twice as much as he had." No more to be dry, thirsty, parched, cracked, split and broken.

When you find yourself walking through a dry and thirsty time. Micah 7:5-8 "Trust not in a friend, put you not confidence in a guide: keep the doors of your mouth from her (your wife) that lieth in thy bosom. For the son dishonors the father, the daughter rises up against her mother, the daughter in law, against her mother in law; a man's enemies are the men of his own house. THEREFORE, I WILL LOOK UNTO THE LORD; I will wait for the God of my salvation: my God will hear me. (This is a form of Resurrection Power.) Rejoice not against me, O mine enemy: when I fall, I shall arise; when I sit in darkness, the LORD shall be a light unto me." Then and only then will the drops of water begin to fall upon your dry and thirsty soul. It will soften the anger and disappointments in your life.

Then, take a stand Matthew 16:23 "Get thee behind me, Satan: thou art an offence unto me: for thou savourest not the things that be of God, but those that be of men." More drops of water as you stand upon the Word of God.

Matthew 16:25,26 "For whosoever will save his life shall lose it: and whosoever will lose his life for my sake shall find it. For what is a man profited, if he shall gain the whole world, and lose his own soul? Or what shall a man give in exchange for his soul?" The soul is our mind, will and emotions. What will we gain if we gain our quest for money, fame, and power but lose our mind, will and emotional stability in the process?

Luke 12:7 "And even the very hairs of your head are all numbered. Fear not therefore: you are of more value than many sparrows." Remember, don't fear but stand in faith for you are more valuable than not one, but many sparrows.

John 6:63 "It is the spirit that quickeneth; the flesh profiteth nothing the words that I speak (Jesus) unto you, they are spirit, and they are life." Jesus' words of truth bring life to us.

Colossians 3:16 "Let the word of Christ dwell in you richly in all wisdom; teaching and admonishing one another in psalms and hymns and spiritual songs, singing with grace in your hearts to the Lord." Colossians 3:8 "Beware lest any man spoil you through philosophy and vain deceit, after the tradition of men, after the rudiments of the world, and not after Christ." Keep your mind on the words of God, on good things, and don't let anyone who is full of deceit and vanity sway you with their philosophy or you will find yourself still in a dry thirsty place.

Why then do you feel that you are a thirsty dry land where there is not water? Jeremiah 8:5 "Why then is this people of Jerusalem slidden back (turned away) by a perpetual backsliding? They hold fast deceit, they refuse to return." What a word from the Lord. You find yourself not able to go on because you stay in deceit about your situation.

"Many suffer if a man brings you into bondage, or if a man devours you, if a man takes of you, if a man exalts himself, or if a man hits you on the face." This is a reference to II Corinthians 11:20. You sit with no strength.

Ephesians 6:10 "Put on the whole Armour of God, that you may be able to stand against the wiles (trick or lies) of the devil." Ephesians 6:11 "For we wrestle not against flesh and blood, but against principalities, against powers, against the rulers of the darkness of this world, against spiritual wickedness in high places." Stand in truth, righteousness, the gospel of peace, your shield of faith, salvation and the sword of the Spirit, which is the Word of God.

Isaiah 40:29-31 "He gives power to the faint; and to them that have no might, he increases strength. Even the youths shall faint and be weary, and young men shall utterly fall: BUT they that wait upon the Lord shall renew their strength; they shall mount up with wings as eagles; they shall run, and not be weary; and they shall walk, and not faint."

Isaiah 41:17 "When the poor and needy seek water, and there is none, and their tongue faileth for thirst, I the Lord will hear them, I the God of Israel will not forsake them." Standing on the words and truths of God will refresh and strengthen you. When you are in need, God will hear you and He will not turn away from you. You should not give up and give in, but look to God and He will lift you up and be there for you.

CHAPTER 8
My Soul Longs For Thee

God, my soul longs for Thee in a dry and thirsty land.

Psalm 63:1 "O God, thou art my God; early will I seek thee: my soul thirsteth for thee, my flesh longeth for thee in a dry and thirsty land, where no water is;"

This is the beginning of Psalm 63. A Psalm of David, when he was in the wilderness of Judah.

How are you doing these days? Does your mind and emotions scream out saying God, I am thirsty, God, I am dry? David felt the same way. What to do?

The 1st verse stated above shows us that the first thing David did was to acknowledged God; he is truthful with God and states who God is to him. "Thou art my God."

Verse 2 "To see thy power and thy glory, so as I have seen thee in the sanctuary."

Notice David was not anywhere near a sanctuary. He was alone.

Let's jump over to Psalm 42:1-3 "As the hart panteth after the water brooks, so panteth my soul after thee, O God. My soul thirsteth for God, for the living God. When shall I come and appear before God? My tears have been my meat day and night, while they continually say unto me, where is thy God? "

Do you ever feel so terribly alone? Perhaps, there is no church to go to, or other Christians around you that can comfort you. Are you in a desert place in your life? Have you been finding that others are wondering where God is in your state of affairs? Are you ever finding yourself crying out day and night? I believe all of us find ourselves in that type of circumstance sometime in our life. Let's not give up hope....hope thou in God. Let's see what decision David made and learn from him.

Verse 3 of Psalm 63 ..."Because thy loving kindness is better than life, my lips shall praise thee."

My goodness... David decided to praise God in the mist of his circumstance. "I praise you Lord, I praise you Lord." Even better, why not give a sacrifice of praise in song? Oh, you are probably saying, forget it, I don't want to sing. How could you ask me to sing now when I feel so dry and thirsty? Well, let's not forget that, "God inhabits the praises of His people." We can sing and praise God and He will show up for us.

Psalm 63:verse 4..."Thus will I bless thee while I live: I will lift up my hands in thy name."

Can you see David making this decision and statement and lifting up his hands to God?

How wonderful. David decided to have church right where he was.

Why did he decide to do this? What was his purpose? Look at verse 5..."My soul (mind, will and emotions) shall be satisfied as with marrow and fatness; and my mouth shall praise thee with joyful lips:"

When is David intending to do all this? Verse 6 ..."When I remember thee upon my bed, and meditate on thee in the night watches."

Well, it looks to me like every time he remembers God during the day and even through the night, David will be praising God. How about you? How about me? Sounds good to me. It says in the bible, **"Don't give place to the devil."** I guess this would be a really good way to keep your eyes on God.

Why is David doing all this anyway? Verse 7 ..."Because thou hast been my help, therefore in the shadow of thy wings will I rejoice."

Oh, look at that, David is reflecting on the times God had been there for him and drawing strength from past victories. Also, he says, "In the shadow of thy wings will I rejoice." Psalm 91:4...."He (God) shall cover thee with his feathers, and under his wings shalt thou trust: his truth shall be thy shield and buckler." God's truth in your situation shall be a shield to you.

The last verse I will share with you is verse 8. "My soul followeth hard after thee: thy right hand upholdeth me." David now is confessing hope in his situation.

To sum it all up... when we find ourselves in a dry and thirsty place, we need to turn to God. Get under the shadow of His wings and seek God's truth in your situation. Have church any time you think on God, if during the day or at night or both. Just start to praise Him, lift up your hands to Him, and thank Him for all He has done and what He will do for you.

Jesus said, "I will never leave you or forsake you." One of the Old Testament prophets gave a "thus sayeth the Lord", saying... "But, cleave unto the Lord your God, as ye have done unto this day. For the Lord hath driven out from before you great nations and strong but as for you no man hath been able to stand before you unto this day. One man of you shall chase a thousand for the Lord your God, he it is that fighteth for you, as he hath promised you. Take heed therefore, unto yourselves that you love the Lord your God."

CHAPTER 9

Child of God, Why Do You Fear?

This was from God, given to me and also for some of you. So read on and be encouraged.

Child of God, why do you fear? Don't you know my camp is around you everywhere? This is not a time of pain but joy and unspeakable gain. The waves have calmed and the storm has past and now I draw you close, in my arms of love. Don't you see? Don't you know that I love you with an everlasting love? Sadness flees and love takes hold. This is a time for you to be bold…Bold in my love and showered in grace. A smile will shine upon your face. Don't be saddened by times past. Know that my love will last and last.

I have not given you a spirit of fear. My love for you will adhere. Your walk with me has been shaky and tried, but the shadows of darkness will up and flee. There will be a healing for you, from me. Blessings will come and stay in your life. This will be a time of joy, not strife. If you could see the bright blue sky and the stars that twinkle in the midnight sky, then you would know what I say is true. This will be a new time of joy, brand new. So don't worry and don't fret. This is the best time yet. My mercy will flow from my throne on high. The crying will stop and you'll not even know why.

My Mercy will fall like a soft gentle snow. It will permeate your being, with songs of love, you will be singing. Showers of blessing are on the horizon, so be sure to thank me for every one. Daylight is coming and you'll know the truth. Meditate in my Word and be renewed and let my words speak to you of me. Clouds may form but they are not of me.

All will be brighter, you will see. So, stop all your worry and fear and fret and be ready for a better time yet. Stop all the fussing and sit still, and know that I am God and then do my will. Peace, prosperity, fun and games, laughing and joking will make a claim. So stop all the fussing and stand still and know that I am God.... And Do My Will.

When you have done all you can do, stand therefore in the liberty of God and don't be entangled again in this yoke of bondage.

CHAPTER 10

When Nobody Cares, God Is There

Have you ever found yourself wandering on the streets of despair, looking for someone, anyone who would care? Did the darkness surround you like falling rain, feeling lonelier and lonelier, searching in vain?

Why has it happened? What has brought this on? You feel so lonely, yet love can't be found. Why all this dread and fear and doubt? Why do you feel all left out?

No Hope??? **"Hope thou in God"**, the bible declares. "Faith is the substance of things hoped for, and the evidence of things not yet seen." When there is no hope, turn to God for He speaks those things that are not as though they were. (Romans 4:13-17)

What has the enemy stolen from you? Is it joy, peace, love, or possibly a quiet spirit?

How has this happened? What have you done that you should repent? Let us seek within ourselves for the lies that separate us from our Father in heaven. Let us take this time to repent of our wrong doings. What... I can hear you saying, " My wrong doings? You don't know what they did to me. You just don't know." It doesn't matter what they did to you. What matters is how you react to what they did to you.

God tells us to forgive. Why, because if we don't forgive, we find ourselves constantly in a battle. Our nerves get shot and we start looking for things to relax us. We shake and quiver and get angry and scream, hurting others around us. Forgive and your peace will return to you. Forgive and your nerves will be strengthened again. Forgive and you'll find God's mercy and grace.

Jesus says, "I will never leave you or forsake you." What do you say? "I'll be right back Jesus, as soon as I take care of this problem." Jesus says, "Come unto me, all ye that are weary and heavy laden and I will give you rest." And you say, "I'll get rested, then I'll be right there with you Jesus."

How sad to think we can work things out on our own, when God says, "The heart is desperately wicked and deceitful above all things, who can know it". "Many are the afflictions of the righteous, but God delivers them from them all."

We need to be seeking God's wisdom always in our situations. Then and only then will we be able to find true peace, forgiveness and joy. Remember, the joy of the Lord is our strength.

Shouldn't we start a new time in our life, filled with the peace of God, the joy of knowing Him and the relief of forgiveness toward others and ourselves? How can you be a truly useful minister of His word and have a more blessed life, if you don't start afresh?

Let's not miss a chance for our relationship with the Father to be restored. Let's go on and redeem the time. Let's go on with our Father's business and be a blessing to others.

CHAPTER 11
The Flesh & The Spirit

Isn't it strange how we do things we shouldn't do and wish we did the things that were pleasing to God? I'm sure you are familiar with the passage in the bible about this very same thing. How the flesh and the Spirit war against each other. (Galatians Chapter Five) Who will deliver us from this problem? (Romans Chapter Six) Who will help us out, Jesus of course.

I was watching "Touched By An Angel" a while back and realized that Monica was so saddened by the trials of life that she felt she had to go away from God and be alone in a desert place. Have you ever felt that way? There you are thinking you are going off all alone to work out your problem(s). And yet, you find you are becoming more confused than when you started out, if that is possible.

Now you sit thinking you are alone, wandering, wandering. Guess what! You are not. Just like Monica in "Touched By An Angel" was not alone. She found herself being tempted by the devil. Of course, he looked like a man, but she knew different. How are the deceptions played out? Let's look at a few.

> ... You are down. What do you need? a kind word, a hug, drugs, or someone just to say, "I understand".... And what can you find? deception at the door. How, through a stranger who doesn't know God?

A DRY AND THIRSTY LAND

Through close well-meaning friends who either don't know God, or like Jobs friends, who didn't understand?

That's right! Deception, to help you to stay away from God and pulling you further into confusion or just keeping you bound. It's all so easy for you to miss God when you walk away to figure it out on your own.

Well, back to the story of Monica. She was in the wilderness, a desert place. There she was being persuaded to just jump off a cliff into the arms of, seemingly, a friend, which of course, he was not. All of a sudden, she calls out to God and says "God I want to be with you. Forgive me". There in the midst of her trial, in her desert experience, a plant full of flowers bloom God heard her cry and was there for her.

God will hear our cry. He will never leave us or forsake us, even though we sometimes forsake him. How sad that is for us.

In your wilderness or desert experience, God will answer you if you only cry out to him with your heart. Just like Monica, I found myself in a dry and thirsty land where no water was, spiritually. What had happened? I too decided to try and work it out on my own.

Finally, just like Monica, I cried out to God and he answered me. He showed me that He was with me. How? Through sunsets of magnificent beauty... by a beautifully breathtaking moonlit night....through the beauty of the sky in the evening before sunset...a multitude of birds which hardly could be numbered ...and so much more.

God has not forgotten you either. He can make a way where there is no way and paths where there are no paths. He can turn your darkness into light and make you smile once again. You

MARILYN MARINELLI

need only to turn to Him with your whole heart and follow Him as he leads you day-by-day and moment-by-moment.

Jesus said, **"I am the way, the truth and the life**." Isaiah records these words, **"No weapon formed against you shall prosper."**

> In the midst of your confusion, I am there
> to wipe away your every care.
> I sit beside you everyday
> hoping you'd reach out
> so I can show you the way.

I pray God will reveal Himself to you and that you will turn your problems and concerns over to Him.

CHAPTER 12
Mattress or Faith

Troubled on every side, and sadness looming at the door of our hearts. Cares and concerns fear and doubt pulling at our very fiber. Hang on hang on dear children of God for He has not given us a spirit of fear but of power and love and a sound mind.

"But, I'd rather fear.... It is so strong a pull on my flesh." Yes, we have all been there and still do feel its pull on us. Wait.... What are you doing in the flesh??? We are to walk by faith not by sight. We are to walk in the Spirit and not the flesh.

Let me tell you a story. Of course, you may find it humorous because it wasn't you. We had just moved to Wisconsin and the springtime had come. How lovely it was. Not to me, because the threats of tornadoes were all around. "Haven't you heard?" "Don't you know? That tornadoes are a reality here in Wisconsin?" "Oh no!" I thought--"TORNADOES!" Fear struck my heart. What will I do????? What a great Christian response huh?

My faith up and fled when I found myself one afternoon seeing the report to take shelter.

Warning! Warning! was the report. Take the necessary precautions as reports for a possible strike of a tornado screamed across the television screen.

I quickly ran downstairs to the basement. Sure, I thought, where is my husband at work of course. Couldn't this warning come at a time when my husband was home? After all, how can I handle this alone?

What to do, I pulled the mattress from the other side of the basement to the Southwest corner. It's supposed to be safer there. So there I was a little bitsy thing dragging a full size mattress across the basement floor. Oh no the sky is black...the storm is here. The trees are swaying and the thunder screaming and the lighting striking.

Cowering in fear behind the mattress, I prayed. "Jesus help calm the storm, protect me."

"Jesus you calmed the storm in the bible story I read. Please do it now for me."

Then I heard Jesus speak to my heart. "You speak to the storm. I can do it, but I gave you the authority to speak to the storms in your life." Thanks a lot Jesus, I thought. Now I have to do it little old whimpy me. Obedience, that's all I had going for me. I will walk by faith and not by sight and be obedient to what Jesus told me to do.

So there I was hiding behind my mattress. I peeked out and pointed my finger and with authority spoke to the storm to stop in the name of Jesus and then quickly hid behind the mattress again. Within a few minutes the storm had ceased.

Well, I certainly learned a lesson. Because of my fear, I pulled my back out from dragging that mattress all over the basement and had to go to the chiropractor. There you go. See what happens when you respond to things around you through the flesh? But standing in the Spirit, the storm ceased.

I have prayed against many storms since then. We lived in Wisconsin for 7 years and believe me I had a lot of practice.

A DRY AND THIRSTY LAND

One thing more, the Lord gave me His Word that I could stand on during all those years. It was Psalm 91 "He that dwells in the secret place of the Most High shall abide under the shadow of the Almighty. And I will say of the Lord He is my strength and my refuge." You can read the rest for yourself. It will build your faith.

We since moved away from Wisconsin. A few years after we left, my very good friend who had lived across the street from me called and said that a tornado had hit the area. The roof of her home was damaged that the house across the street where we had lived was affected as well. God's protection was there for our home because I stood on God's Word.

Since that time, they now say that the safest side of the basement is the Southeast not the Southwest. Goes to show you, you can't rely on man. It's better to be obedient to God's direction for your life.

Well, maybe you got a little chuckle out of my experience. But, what about your concerns, doubts and fears? How are you handling it? God's word says, "I have not given you a spirit of fear, but of power and love and a sound mind." His word says, "Speak to the mountain to be removed and cast into the sea and not doubt in your heart but believe."

Your obedience to what God shows you to do does not only help you but others around you. If I hadn't been obedient to what Jesus told me to do, in the midst of the storm, my home could have been destroyed. I could have been destroyed and my animals in the home also.

Romans 8:12-39 "Therefore, brethren, we are debtors, not to the flesh, to live after the flesh. For if you live after the flesh, you shall die: but if you through the Spirit do mortify the deeds of the body, you shall live. For as many as are led by the Spirit of God, they are the sons of God. For you have not received the spirit of bondage again to fear; but you have received the Spirit of adoption, whereby we cry, Abba, Father. The Spirit itself beareth witness with our spirit, that we are the children of God: And if children, then heirs; heirs of God, and joint-heirs with Christ: if so be that we suffer with him, that we may be also glorified together. For I reckon that the suffering of this present time are not worthy to be compared with the glory, which shall be revealed in us.

For the earnest expectation of the creature waits for the manifestation of the sons of God. For the creature was made subject to vanity, not willingly but by reason of him who hath subjected the same to hope. Because the creature itself also shall be delivered from the bondage of corruption into the glorious liberty of the children of God. For we know that the whole creation groans and travails in pain together until now. And not only they, but ourselves also, which have the first fruits of the Spirit, even we ourselves groan within our selves waiting for the adoption to wit, the redemption of our body. For we are saved by hope: but hope that is seen is not hope: for what a man seeth, why does he yet hope for?

Likewise the Spirit also helps our infirmities: for we know not what we should pray for as we ought: but the Spirit itself makes intercession for us with groanings which cannot be uttered. And he that searches the hearts knows what is the mind of the Spirit, because he makes intercession for the saints according to the will of God.

And we know that all things work together for good to them that love God, to them who are the called according to his purpose. For whom he did foreknow, he also did predestinate to be conformed to the image of his Son, that he might be the firstborn of among many brethren. Moreover whom he did predestinate, them he also called: and whom he called, them he also justified: and whom he justified, them he also glorified.

What shall we then say to these things? IF GOD BE FOR US, WHO CAN BE AGAINST US?

He that spared not his own Son, but delivered him up for us all how shall he not with him also freely give us all things? Who shall lay any thing to the charge of God's elect? It is God that justifieth. Who is he that condemneth? It is Christ that died, yea rather, that is risen again, who is even at the right hand of God, who also makes intercession for us.

Who shall separate us from the love of Christ? Shall tribulation, or distress, or persecution, or famine, or nakedness, or peril, or sword? As it is written, For thy sake we are killed all the daylong: we are accounted as sheep for the slaughter.

Nay, in all these things we are more than conquerors through him that loved us.

For I am persuaded, that neither death, nor life, nor angels, nor principalities, nor powers, nor things present, nor things to come, nor height nor depth, nor any other creature shall be able to separate us from the love of God, which is in Christ Jesus our Lord."

May your heart be at peace. Be obedient to the Lord's direction in your life. Let your faith stand in the power of God and not in the wisdom of man.

CHAPTER 13
Miracles Still Happen

There are many miracles recorded in the bible. But you say how about today? Some people can tell you first hand what they have seen or experienced and others still have doubts. Well, miracles still happen. That is if you believe God.

I am going to share with you some miracles in my life in hopes that it will strengthen your faith.

A number of years ago a man approached me at a Christian meeting, **Pipe Line To Jesus**. The man handed me a dollar bill and said, " I want you to have this dollar bill. It has all 7's on it, representing perfection. You will be receiving a miracle." Then he laid hands on me and I went down under the power of God. Even though my husband tried to pick me up, I couldn't move.

About a year or so later, I was injured by a chiropractor. It's a very long story and a very long time of healing. I won't go into to much detail at this time. I will tell you that I lost the ability to feel in my left arm; my eyesight in my left eye was very poor and I wasn't getting enough blood flow to my head on the left side. One of my bones in my back had moved out of place and was hitting upon a nerve and damaging it. My muscles in my neck, shoulder and back area were frozen. The chiropractor that had caused this had checked me out and told me I was all right. But, his masseuse told me there was a bone out of place. Well, I was a mess. I had another appointment with a new chiropractor. It was going to take a few weeks because he was on vacation.

I prayed and sought the Lord. I applied the Word of God concerning healing and thanked the Lord for His healing touch. As the days passed, I was in a lot of pain. One morning I woke up and remembered I once read in a Kenneth Copeland magazine that I need to receive my healing. So while lying in bed that morning, as I awoke in pain, I said out loud, **"I receive my healing right now in the name of Jesus."** I meant it with all I had in me.

No sooner did I say it, a sharp pain went through my back where the bone had been out of place. I felt the bone move back into place. When I went to the new chiropractor, he took an x-ray of my back. My bone was not out of place. God showed me in His Word that He would renew me like the noonday and the morning and that He would strengthen me. It took seven months for me to feel normal again. Remember the man and the dollar bill with the sevens on it, which meant perfection. God had perfected me in 7 months. My miracle had taken place. God shared many scriptures with me throughout these seven months. I stood on new words from God each day. The one that I stood on first was **"Daughter your faith has made you whole. Go in peace and be healed of this plague."** Let God's Word be true. No one knew but God, what had really happened to me.

God also answered a prayer about meeting Oral Roberts. My shoulder was still freezing up on me, no matter how many massages I would have. My faithful husband massaged me everyday and the massage therapist would came every other week or so. Oral Roberts was to speak at a local church and we went to see him. After Oral Roberts gave his message he said, "I don't understand this but God is telling me that someone here has a frozen shoulder and He is healing you. Will you stand up;" That was me. After that day my shoulder never froze up again. Praise God.

There are so many great things God has done for me. I could write a book on them alone.

Let me tell you what happened to a lady who was going to a small ladies fellowship. She had some work done on several veins in her legs. She had some complications and now was faced with going back to the doctor again. She really was dreading the visit. She had asked the woman who had ministered that day to pray for her. The woman told her that when she prayed earlier in the meeting for another lady, it was also for her.

The Lord spoke to me and told me I needed to pray for her. Lord, I said, I have a headache and want to go home. If you really want me to pray for Cindy then let us meet somehow. Well I proceeded to leave the home and as I did Cindy got up from the couch and wound up right in front of me. I said, "Cindy do you want me to pray for you?" She said yes, so I got on my knees, put my hand on her leg, where the problem was, and said; **"I speak to this clot in the vein and command it to dissolve, in the name of Jesus. Thank you God. Amen."** Then I said goodbye to Cindy and left.

The following week I went to church. Who was sitting in back of me? It was Cindy and her husband. She told me she went back to the doctor for her appointment and the vein was fine. That night she gave her life to the Lord.

Where is your faith for a miracle?

A lady I didn't know was at church one day sitting in a wheel chair. Many people knew her. Some of the people in church started to pray for her. As she was brought passed me. I prayed for her. Two years later, I ran into this same woman at a Christian Ladies meeting. She remembered me...grabbed me and said,

I remember you. After you prayed for me that day, I have been walking...not great but I have been walking. Praise God.

I just hope that you will rejoice with me for these precious times. Know that God loves you and wants you well. He will always make a way where there is no way and paths where there are no paths. I pray that these testimonies will build your faith.

Heavenly Father, we come to you in the name of Jesus, the name that is above all names. We ask you Lord to touch your people. Minister to the broken hearted; uplift the broken in spirit; refresh their souls. Father, In Jesus name, make them whole and well and blessed of you.

We take authority over sickness and disease and release the healing power of Jesus upon all who need healing knowing that, "He was wounded for our transgression, bruised for our iniquities and the chastisement of our peace was laid upon Him; and by his stripes we were healed." We pray right now that the blood of Jesus will cleanse them from all unrighteousness. Thank you Father that you have heard our prayers. We wait expectantly upon you.

CHAPTER 14
Lost But Not Forgotten

Did you ever feel lost? God has not forgotten you. He says in His word, "Behold, I have engraved you in the palm of my hand." Don't you know you are more precious that silver or gold? Don't you know that you are more important than the sparrow? **God has not forgotten you**. You are precious in His sight.

Verily, verily I say unto you; unless a grain of wheat fall to the ground, it will abide alone. It will stay the same, never changing, never growing into what it really was intended to be. If you sit still and not move on, you stay the same. Each day becomes like the one before. Your life becomes like a barren field. Nothing is there to warm the soul. As people pass by, they don't see the real you or the glory of God placed in your heart and mind. Instead they see nothing but a barren wasteland.

How can you change? How can you grow? Plant yourself in good soil. Plant yourself back in the Word of God. Let God's Word water you. Let praise fall from your lips. Drink! Drink! Drink! And Drink some more. Let the Word wash your soul. In time, you will see God move within you. You will spring up with fruit that you can share with others. The ground of your heart will become moist with the presence of God. Then you will find your true self. Then and only then will you be ready to be used of God, as He has intended for you to be.

"Mark the perfect man and behold the upright man for the end of that man is peace." How does this man get peace? By giving his life to Jesus. How often do we think that we can never walk away from our walk with God? And yet, through some simple ways, ways that we don't even realize we are doing, we find ourselves lost in a barren wasteland looking for water. Maybe, we just stopped seeking God through our reading of His Word, thinking that it's all right and that we're doing just fine. After all, look at all the times I've read the Word. Or maybe you helped someone so much that you lost your own way. Whatever the cause was, I believe that God wants us to know that as we look to Him that water will begin to flow on our barren field and just like the rain refreshes the trees and flowers so God's Word can refresh our lives once again.

Don't give up now. "As the deer pants for the water, so my soul longs after thee."

Seek and you shall find, knock and the door shall be open to you. The battlefield is your mind. Don't let your mind be dormant with the things of the past; Things you can't fix. Fight the good fight of faith. Stand fast and know that I am God." Resist the devil and he will flee from you."

Water me Lord with your love.
Shower me with your Words from above.
Fill me Lord with your mercy and grace,
That I may behold your face.
Help me to grow and help me to see,
The wonder you have worked in me.

Written By
Marilyn Marinclli

CHAPTER 15

Close The Doors And Walk On

Jesus said," I have come to give you life and to give it to you more abundantly." "The devil comes to steal, kill and destroy." (John 10:10) Are you walking in sadness and grief or sorrow and despair?

Where are you? What doors have you opened? If you answer these questions, you will know where and why you are walking the way you are.

But I didn't do anything, you say. Yes, you did, because you have a will and a choice to keep what you want in your life. You and only you can make the choice. You can choose to follow God if you want to. God will help you through, if you confess and call upon Jesus and use the blood of Jesus to defeat your circumstances.

CALL upon the NAME of JESUS

"CAST down every imagination and every high thing that exalts itself against the knowledge of God, and bring into captivity every thought to the obedience of Christ, when your obedience is fulfilled." (II Corinthians: 10:4-7)

Now Hear The Word of The Lord To You Today

"The Blood of Jesus cleanses you from all unrighteousness." (I John 1:9) "The weapons of your warfare are not carnal but mighty, through Christ. To the pulling down of strongholds." "No weapon formed against you shall prosper and every tongue that rises up against you in judgment you shall be condemned."

"Fight the good fight of faith for verily, verily I say unto you that you are the children of God and joint heirs. The just shall live by faith."

What doors have you opened? Look around and see who's residing in the rooms of your heart and emotions.

Isaiah 35:8-10 "And a highway shall be to them and a way, and it shall be called, "The way of Holiness" The unclean shall not pass over it, but it shall be there for those: the wayfaring men, the fools shall not ere therein. No lion shall be there, or ravenous beast shall go up thereon, it shall not be found there; but the redeemed shall walk there:

And the ransomed of the Lord shall return and come to Zion with songs and everlasting joy shall be upon their heads: they shall obtain joy and gladness, and sorrow and sighing shall flee away."

Romans 9:35-39 "Who shall separate us from the love of Christ? Shall tribulation, or distress, or persecution, or famine or nakedness, or peril, or sword? As it is written, For thy sake we are killed all the day long; we are accounted as sheep for the slaughter.

NAY, in all these things we are more than conquerors through him that loved us.

For I am persuaded that neither death, nor life, nor angels, nor principalitities nor powers, nor things present, nor things to come. Nor height, nor depth, nor any other creature, shall be able to separate us from the love of God which is in Christ Jesus our Lord."

I Corinthians 15:22 "For as in Adam all die, even so in Christ shall all be made alive."

John 5:24 "Verily, verily, I say unto you, He that heareth my word, and believeth on him that sent me, hath everlasting life, and shall not come into condemnation; but is passed from death unto life."

Romans12:2 "And be not conformed to this world; but be ye transformed by the renewing of your mind that ye may prove what is that good and acceptable, and perfect, will of God."

II Corinthians 5:7 " For we walk by faith, not by sight."

John 16:33 "These things I have spoken unto you that in me you might have peace. In the world, ye shall have tribulation, but be of good cheer: I have overcome the world."

So, if God be for you, who can be against you? He will make a way in your wilderness, and new paths for you to walk. Be encouraged and know that He will never leave you or forsake you. All you need to do is look at the circumstance, reach out to Jesus, and follow the new path provided for you. It takes courage, determination, and applying your faith in what God reveals to you. **Apply! Apply! Apply!**

Don't give up and let the old sit in your heart. Renew yourself and be the person God has created you to be. Forget everyone else and set your face like a flint on God and His Word, and you will find yourself renewing your mind, standing in God's righteousness. You will see the old fade into the past where it belongs. "For behold, I set before you this day truth and strength. I have long time held my peace but now I say shine, stand forth in the liberty of Christ (The "Anointed One" and His anointing)… and do not be entangled again in the yoke of bondage, but be renewed in your spirit and shine forth."

CHAPTER 16
To Share In His Love

Love not the things of this world for they are temporal. Neither look for love from others that are searching as you are. Love streams down from God's hand to the ones that seek Him with all their hearts. He touches them deep within.

God's love permeates the longing soul. His love is shed abroad within the heart of man to touch the lives of others. God uses our hands to sooth someone's aching back or bring a touch in a handshake and so much more. Our eyes express care and love to another. Our ears are used to listen to the needs or sorrow of a hurting heart. **YES, LOVE IS MUCH MORE THAN A FEELING**. Love brings joy to our hearts as God touches us with His love. And yet, we in return share His love with others.

To Share In His Love

I got up this morning to praise you,
Oh, Most High.
Look! I got up to praise you
My God, Most High.

I was ordered by your Spirit,
From your throne above,
To worship and praise you
And give you my love.

The showers of mercy,
That flow from your throne,
Encircles my heart,
And leads me never to roam.

For in the silence
Of your enduring love,
I wake up this morning,
To share in your love.

Written By
Marilyn Marinelli

True love stands the test of time. There is no such thing as... I love you and then... forget it. God's love is always there. Jesus said, "I will never leave you or forsake you".

Have you been looking for love in all the wrong places? God's love never fails because God is love. Don't be deceived to think that God has left you because other people have. Don't think He hasn't heard your cry for help. Look to Jesus! He is waiting for you to come back to Him. As you take a step towards Him, He will be there for you with outstretched hands, to help heal the hurts within. He will strengthen you. He will uphold you with the right hand of His righteousness. How do I know? Jesus has done it for me. When I thought and felt all was but lost, I heard a minister say, "Jesus is there with outstretched hands, waiting for you."

As I took hold of this, I made my move to reach out in earnest to Jesus. What happened? Jesus met me with joy. So much joy flowed over me that I found myself laughing and laughing out loud. You know, Jesus restored my joy that very moment. I found that Jesus gave me just what I needed, joy and the ability to love again.

MARILYN MARINELLI

Try it. Reach out to Jesus again with all your heart and see what He will do for you.

My prayer is that your focus be, not on who gives you a Valentine card, but rather on the love of God that is shed abroad in your heart. Reach out to Him and see how full you get. Then you too will receive the joy and love that no money can buy; that will last more than just one day in February.

God Is Love

CHAPTER 17
Dealing With A Critical Spirit

"The weapons of our warfare are not carnal but mighty though God to the pulling down of strongholds." What are these weapons? They certainly aren't who can yell the loudest, or who is the physically stronger one. It is rather a spiritual battle. So then, what are these weapons? They are the armor of God (Ephesians 6:12-18).

Putting on the full armor of God is your best weapon. His armor includes: the breast plate of righteousness, the helmet of salvation, the sword of the spirit, your feet shod with the preparation of the gospel of peace, your loins girt about with the truth and the sword of the Spirit. These are weapons we must use to stand fast in the liberty in which Christ has set us free. Free from what? From deception, critical spirits and so much more.

But, let's take for instance the critical spirit. How do we over come this one?

1. Through our knowing first that we are saved.

2. That God loves us so much that the criticism can roll off our back when we are confronted with it. Why? Because we have searched God's Word and have found out that He accepts us.

3. That if there is anything not right with us, that God will show us what it is so that we can change.

I am reminded of a time that I saw a very old car in front of mine. It had a sticker on it that said something about Jesus. I thought," why would someone be so happy to ride around in this very old car and yet give the praise to Jesus for it?" This was many years ago. But I wasn't riding in the most expensive car, yet it was much better that the one I saw. The Holy Spirit quickened me and reminded me of when I was saved, how everything didn't look as good on the outside either.

Remember, He prompted me. God works from the inside out. Maybe this person didn't have a car at all and they had one now and it was very much a blessing. After all, it is better than trying to walk everywhere. Maybe this was all the person could afford at that time and God was providing for them with this particular car, until the persons faith grew stronger.

We need to be thankful for what we have and take care of the things we have now, not wait for better and then believe we will take care of something better later. If you can't keep an old car clean, why would you keep a beautiful new car clean? Oh, because then you can show it off. I don't think so. God told me years ago to take care of what I had and not to be looking at everything everybody else had that was better. Take the time to be proud of what you have.

So let's not be critical of someone else that is trying to follow God. And let's take care of the things God has entrusted to us.

Now let's back to Chapter 17 and talk a bit more on being criticized. You know, when someone criticized me, I would fall apart. But, God showed me a better way. I should keep my eyes on Him and know that God is guiding me. Do you know what happened? God built me up, made me stronger through His Word, as I sought Him and read my bible. Then I even became more knowgeable and was able to stand against criticism.

Not everyone is you and you are not everyone else. All flowers are not the same, yet each one of them is beautiful or handsome in their own way. Wouldn't it be boring if there were only one kind of flower? Look at all we would miss. God has made each and every one of us special and unique. When you let God's love and gifts shine through you, all that you are in God will shine through and be a blessing to others.

How do we stop the critics? By being who you are in God. If you don't know who you are in Him, keep seeking God for your special gifts and talents. You will be surprised at how the critics will find someone else to criticize when you have your shield of faith up to quench their fiery darts.

May God bless you and kept you and let His face shine upon you and give you peace, Peace of mind and peace in your spirit, for all to see that you are blooming for God. What a blessing you will be to others, who are just waiting to enjoy all you have for them that have been given to you by God.

CHAPTER 18
Don't Let Others Keep You Bound

Do you go to a church? What denomination are you? Didn't you feel the anointing at church? Why are you not sitting in the bible study? Don't you want to learn anything?

Let's take… do you go to a church?

Churches are important. They are a welcoming to all those that have gone astray or not saved as yet. Churches, or should I correctly say a building built by people. We all know that the church is made up of the children of God. So do not forsake the gathering of yourselves. "Where two or more are gathered, there am I in the midst of them", Jesus said.

Pastors need the help of others who know God and are anointed in special areas to minister to the lost, the newly saved Christians and younger Christians. So… are you involved in a church to minister to others? Or are you called by God to be in a specific church to grow and learn and be used to then minister to others?

If you don't go to church, why not? Does God not anoint the preaching? Are the songs being sung more like entertainment than corporate worship? Aren't we all supposed to praise and worship God and come into His presence in one accord?

It says in the bible, when they were all in one accord, then the presence of God was there and the ministers could not even stand because of the anointing. Where is that in your church? Where is the anointing at worship time? Who is in charge of the music at your church? Are they someone who plays the piano better than anyone else or can lead music? But are they truly anointed of God to lead others into the throne room of God?

Where is your minister really? If you find yourself saying, well one day he will be a really good minister, then why are you sitting under his teaching? Did they say that about Moses? Or Jesus????? Isn't a minister supposed to be seasoned in the Word and in his relationship with God? Check it out in the bible. **The answer is yes.**

What denomination are you? Oh my, really, you mean you really believe that? We all have been taught differently, yet there is one thread that binds us and that is the true meaning of salvation and the trinity. What denomination are you? I was asked after I was saved and you know what, I couldn't tell you. Why? Because I accepted the Lord in my living room and read and read my bible and applied His Word to my life. God didn't tell me, "You are now of this denomination." He welcomed me into His family and loved me. Denominational choices are yours to make. Make them wisely and with some knowledge from God in His Word.

Do you know what the anointing in church should be? Or.... Are you just going along with others? "Oh the anointing is so strong. Don't you feel it?" as this is announced from the pulpit or music minister. "Do you feel it?????? Well, do you???" The anointing is a touch from God and you will know it when He touches you. You won't be overtaken in the frenzy of the music. Instead, you will be touched by the words and music as the Holy Spirit ministers to your soul. You may cry, rejoice, be ministered to by the words, be healed, and yes, even slain in the Spirit. Only an anointed individual or individuals playing the music can usher in the presence of God, not people that can play extremely well and get you in frenzy.

Why aren't you sitting in a bible study? I have been asked that a number of times. First of all, I have been in a bible study for 22 years, sitting at the master's feet, reading the Word of God and applying it in my life. I am also a Rhema Graduate. Why have I left some bible studies? Because there have been a number of people teaching that weren't teaching at all. Their focus was to socialize and just skim over some teaching. No one was leaving edified. One bible study I was in, the teacher who was the pastor's son, just made a lot of jokes about everything. He turned out to be backslidden and after ministering to him, he went back a stronger Christian and serious about the study. The other long time bible study students couldn't make fun anymore. They had to get serious or leave.

Let me share a story about another women's group that I had attended. The teacher, leading the class, by letting everyone give answers but she never gave the bible answers. She just allowed everyone to believe what they wanted. She had a big class and people came for years. Why? I believe these folks never opened their bible to see what the Word had to say. Why else would they go to such an unfruitful class? Socialize? Be careful from whom you receive teaching. Just because someone says they are a bible teacher, check it out a little further and be smart.

Don't stay away from church or bible study. Always stay in the Word. God will always, through the Holy Spirit, teach you and guide you and give you the answers sometimes others cannot. Or you may not want to share something with others because they may not understand and could lead you astray. But, you can always count on Jesus and His Word. You will know when the bible study or pastor's teaching is right. Check it out with the bible itself. Read before and after scriptures that have been shared to get a full meaning of what is being taught. Sometimes pastors will take them out of contexts to make their point but the point is wrong, at least with that scripture(s). Study the Word. We are told to do so in the bible itself.

Don't let others keep you bound in fear that you are not worthy or lack the knowledge. Let God open the doors for you and rejoice in the Lord and He will give you the desires of your heart. Again I say rejoice, for your heavenly Farther knows what you need. He will never leave you or forsake you. He will stick closer to you than a brother.

Remember, confusion is not of God. Don't be swayed by crowds going in one direction, because, Jesus may be leading you in another.

"Why are thou disquieted oh my soul, hope though in God."

Thank you God for bringing me out of confusion and filling me with knowledge from your throne on high, for I was lost but now I am found. I was blind but now I see.

Be strong and in the power of His might and He will lift you up, for there is healing in His wings. It is not by might, nor by power, but by my spirit sayeth the Lord.

"For though your times were tough and hard and many stones were in your path, I have found you and held your hand and strengthen you in my love. So do not fear or fret or strain within your soul", says the Lord.

The Lord is near to All who call on Him.

Psalm 145:18

CHAPTER 19
Godly Counsel

The Spirit of the Lord is upon me for He has anointed me to preach the gospel to the poor; to give beauty for ashes; to break the bonds that are holding you down. Be set free in Jesus name.

Don't sit in the old stuff any longer. Reach out your hand to Jesus and let Him lift you up. Give thanks in all things and be not entangled again in the yoke of bondage. But, be set free in Jesus name.

There has no temptation taken you that the Lord will not make a way of escape if…You will call out to him and repent…. cry if you have to but truly repent and see the hand of God move in your life.

Be a testimony of what God can and will do for you. If you look to the right and to the left and not to God, you will find yourself stumbling and falling. Haven't we all had enough of that?

God has been there for me in the darkest, darkest, darkest night and yet one thing I did was to say, "I remember what you have done for me in the past. I will not let go of you, even though I can't see you, feel you, or touch you…even though I don't feel like reading the bible, hearing preachers or singing songs." One thing I will do is pray to not let go of that one beam of light I have from you God.

God has helped me through but I needed to heed His directions. Didn't matter how difficult it was, I still needed to press through. Are you waiting on someone else to help you? Forget it! They do not really know the depths of despair that you are going through. They will give you kind words, may pray and some of the pastors just don't have the time.

It says in the bible, "If you will seek me (God) with all you heart then...

We all need to have a relationship with the Lord. Oh, don't tell me you do if you really don't. How many times have you sought the Lord and He answered you through His Word (the bible.)? How many days did you stand (when you have done all to do then stand therefore)? Stand, stand, stand on the Word God has given you in your prayer time and don't let it go. I say again, don't let anyone sway you from what God said. If you don't listen and obey, you will never see the Divine hand of God in your life. You will never see what great and mighty things God will do for you. Don't let anyone change your mind.

I have seen the love and mercy of God upon my life. The Lord, through His Word, the bible, in prayer has answered me. Not just one scripture but sometimes many scriptures tied together as if someone was always having a conversation with me. It is great. Don't say I can't. Don't say I won't. Say, I will. "For God so loved the world that He gave His only begotten Son that whosoever believes in Him shall not perish but have everlasting life." Start now. If you feel like you are just going to burst and not be able to make it through...pray. No maybe you can't make it through, but God can make a way where there is no way and a path where there is no path.

MARILYN MARINELLI

I feel led of the Lord to pray for you. Why because I make my declaration of faith that all things work together for good to those that love the Lord and are called according to His purpose. (Romans 8:28)

Don't sit around waiting for things to change. Seek God in your circumstance and He will lead you through. It is not enough for you to cry. Crying will not move the hand of God.

But, seeking Him with all your heart and standing on what He tells you to do will move mountains.

It is not enough for you to go to church and cry to the pastor. You need your personal walk with the Lord. For He will never leave you or forsake you but will bring you through and give you peace.

I pray that you are blessed and that things will begin to change for you as you call upon the Lord and apply His Word to your situation.

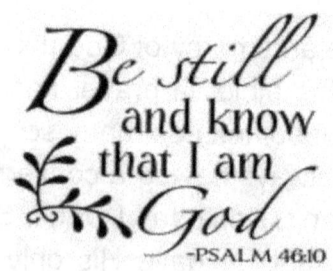

CHAPTER 20

God Is Still Speaking, " Are You Still Listening?"

In the middle of this and that. Did you ever feel yourself sitting in between two ways in which to walk, the old and familiar and the new that is possibly more exciting?

The old and familiar feels like a comfortable shoe. The new, however, is exciting, unknown, and fun to wear. Some of our circumstances in life bring about the best in us. Others, well, they just wash away our smiles, enthusiasm and joy. I think we have all felt that way as we walk through life. Even as I observed our two dogs, sometimes they wake up filled with such joy and excitement and other times they get up slowly and wander outside. What makes the difference?

What I have observed from our dogs is the excitement they express related to the questions that I ask them. They look and wonder, "Are we going with you today?" Or "Do we stay home?" If I say, "Want to go for a walk or a ride in the van? They jump with joy and run all over the house barking and barking, running and leaping with excitement and joy. If they see me get dressed and I don't say a word, they wonder and hang around just waiting for the words ride or walk. If I say, "I'm going to the store", they just look as if to say, "Oh all right, guess we are not going anywhere." They don't realize they are better off at home but they respect me anyway. But when I do tell them to come with me, they are protected by me, even if they think they have it all together.

Why are you telling me about your dogs? Isn't this supposed to be a teaching on my relationship with God? Well, keep your shirt on.

How many times do you find yourself praying and seeking God for a way? Which way should I precede in a situation? Why is it that though, with all my heart, I want to go this way, yet you show me in your Word and prayer time that I must stay put? How many times has God told you to do something and you stayed put and should have moved on? Or, you moved on when God told you to stay put?

I heard a teaching on Elisha. When God told him to go by the brook Cherith and the ravens would bring him food. He needed to stay beside a brook so that water would be available to him. (I Kings 17:1-4) Don't you think he would have rather been in a nice cozy comfortable spot that was familiar?

What was going to happen to him anyway sitting by the brook? But he stayed right there. He had just prophesied to Ahab and told him that a drought would come. Guess what? God placed Elisha in the right spot where he could find water so he wouldn't thirst and food would be delivered to him twice a day by ravens.

Elisha could have complained and said, this is not a good enough provision, God. But, he had time to rest and relax and the stream of water was there any time he needed a drink. The ravens were his servants, bringing him food everyday. What a time. Wouldn't you like to relax and be served? So what if the servants looked like birds, who cares?

And there at the brook, Elisha sat no friends, no TV, nothing but the sound of the brook and nature all around him. After the brook dried up, Elisha was told of God to leave that place and go and see a widow lady for his provision. (I Kings 17:9) And so Elisha obeyed and was provided food and water once again. Remember there was a drought throughout the land. But, God took care of Elisha and when the widow woman helped, she also was taken care of.

What if Elisha was stubborn and didn't want the provisions God had provided for him?

How about, if he responded with anger, hostility, complaining and just flat refused the provisions of God. He would have found himself hungry, thirsty, very sad and probably would have died. Instead he found peace, wasn't thirsty, was fed, even when the brook dried up, God still provided for him. But he had to obey and not rely on what he wanted to do. So, Elisha still went on and was taken care of and helped others along the way and blessed them.

When my puppy dogs, Maggie and Buddy, obey what I ask them to do, they also find provisions. Their water is always available, they always have food, and they are always sitting under the protection of my love. If they didn't, they would wander off on their own, searching for something to eat and something to drink, never finding peace and always searching for comfort and love. As we all know, everyone that they would come across would not treat them so kindly. After all, there are many dangers out there. Good thing they have learned to obey me and respect me. Then they will be protected, provided for and loved. Who wouldn't want to have that? By the way, my dog Buddy just loves watching T.V., especially Animal Planet. He just sits there in an overstuffed chair with his front paws crossed and doesn't have a care in the world. Why? Because, he knows in whom he believes, trusts me and feels safe. I wonder what he is watching right now. Maybe I'd better go look. It could be something good like "Breed All About It", or "Miracle Babies".

Well, how much more will our Father God take care of us if we will seek Him and heed His voice. When God says, **"WALK"** then we walk. When He says, **"STAY",** then we stay. And when He says, **"COME"**, then we come. All the time knowing we are in His care, love and protection.

CHAPTER 21
You Can Still Be A Blessing

Lets go back for a minute to Elisha sitting by the brook being fed by ravens. This time, I would like to go deeper into Elisha's situation. There he had been, standing in a mighty anointing of God, calling fire down from heaven. The next moment, Jezebel was after him to take his life. But, God intervened and took Elisha, despondent, heartbroken, tired, discouraged, in despair and provided for him a safe haven.

Think about it. Have you been doing all you know to do in your walk with God and then all of a sudden this great enemy rises up to destroy you? Did you ever feel like you could not go on? Didn't you ever feel like you just were going to give up? Did you ever feel like God had no more for you to do? Did you ever feel like you were the only one in the whole world standing on God's promises? What went wrong?

Whatever went wrong, God shows us that He has not forgotten us and that He will make provisions for us just like Elisha. As long as we reach out for God, He will not leave us or forsake us. But, instead, He will provide what we need at the time.

Let's look further into what God did for Elisha. There was Elisha feeling beaten, fearful, and seemingly totally alone and forgotten. Then there was God reaching out to him with mercy, grace, forgiveness, care, provision and rest.

Can't you just see Elisha sitting by the brook; the quietness of nature all around him; the stillness of the day, relaxing? Or was he being strengthened in his walk with God, ever growing and being refreshed. Just as the water from the brook refreshes his thirst, so God refreshed Elisha with living water. And the food provided for Elisha was brought to him. Elisha could rest. He didn't have to worry about going to hunt for food. He could just take his ease and rest until his strength and confidence was regained once again and his spirit was filled with faith once more to serve God and bless others.

I have been experiencing that kind of walk. Have you? If not, some time in the future you just might. What will you do? Run, Run, Run or reach out to God for His counsel and help? And when God provides for you, will you find yourself saying something like, "Well, did you have to put me by myself by a brook, stream, lake, beach, etc. and why can't I get the best food at the best stores? Why do I have to go to these local stores where there are just a few people shopping? Why can't I go to the bigger stores to shop for food where many people are?"

Let's look again at Elisha sitting by the brook being taken care of by God. What else was happening? His enemy Jezebel was after him to take his life. But, God took care of that situation while Elisha rested and was restored. Sometimes we want to fight all the battles and yet God says rest, sit back, relax, I will fight for you and move your enemies out of the way.

When we look more closely at Elisha's situation, we see that when the brook dried up, he also was ready with strength in himself and in his relationship with God to go on with his life. God then directed him to a widow woman. She sat with her son, ready to give up her life and his, because of the drought. Elisha shows up at her house with what? Have you guessed it yet?

A DRY AND THIRSTY LAND

Elisha showed up with his strength and his new refreshed walk with God and the anointing and Word of God in him. To do what?... To do for the widow woman what was done for him by God. He first asked her to obey his direction to have faith in him. He then provided for them through God's power. The woman and her son experienced what Elisha had experienced, the provisions of God and hope to go on in life.

Don't you think God can do that for you? Don't you think you have a part to play in someone else's life? It is like a chain reaction. So don't resist when God provides for you in ways that you might not understand. Look around! Are you being provided the rest you need, yet yearning to run, run, run? Take your rest. Be assured that God has not forgotten you. Then you will find yourself filled with the strength of God to go on and be a blessing to others.

Well, God certainly has encouraged me with this teaching. I hope you have been encouraged as well.

CHAPTER 22

Are You Walking In Faith or Under The Law?

Galatians 3:2 "This only would I learn of you, Received ye the Spirit by the works of the law, or by the hearing of faith?" This is the first question God asked me as I sought Him just recently.

The second question was Galatians 3:3 "Are you so foolish? Having begun in the Spirit, are you now made perfect by the flesh?"

Galatians 3:5 is the third question He asked me. "He therefore that ministereth to you the Spirit, and worketh miracles among you, doeth he it by the works of the law, or by the hearing of faith?"

God continued to speak to me through His word Galatians 3:6-9 "Even as Abraham believed God, and it was accounted to him for righteousness. Know ye therefore that they which are of faith, the same are the children of Abraham." And the scripture, foreseeing that God would justify the heathen through faith, preached before the gospel unto Abraham, saying, "In thee shall all nations be blessed." So then they, which be of faith, are blessed with faithful Abraham.

Notice what Galatians 3:10 says, "For as many as are of the works of the law are under the curse; for it is written, Cursed is every one that continueth not in all things which are written in the book of the law to do them." What about Galatians 3:11 & 12? "But that no man is justified by the law in the sight of God, it is evident: for, the just shall live by faith. And the law is not of faith: but, the man that doeth them shall live in them."

The importance of walking in faith is more than we realize. We all seem to say yes we are walking in faith but are we? Let's go on and see what else God showed me.

Galatians 3: 22-26 "But the scripture hath concluded all under sin, that the promise by faith of Jesus Christ might be given to them that believe. But before faith came, we were kept under the law, shut up unto the faith, which should afterwards be revealed. Wherefore the law was our schoolmaster to bring us unto Christ, that we might be justified by faith. But after that faith is come, we are no longer under a schoolmaster. For ye are all the children of God by faith in Christ Jesus."

I would hope, as you can see by now, it is only through faith in Jesus that we are children of God and not because of our works. Where are we going with all this you may be asking?

We are to examine ourselves by what God just showed us. Are you trying to live up to others expectations in church, at bible study, or at any other meeting of a Christian nature? Know that when you accepted Jesus and gave your life to Him that it was by faith not of works. Where are you today? Have you found yourself hindered by others in the Christian community? The following is a question to us from God.

Galatians 5:7 & 8 "Ye did run well; who did hinder you that you should not obey the truth? This persuasion (belief) comes not of him that called you." Galatians 5:9 "A little leaven leaveneth the whole lump."

Have you been walking in the Spirit by faith and someone or many others have, because of their persuasions, caused you to trip up and start walking in the flesh? Or shall I say challenged your authority and caused you to question your walk with the Lord, thereby, causing you to stumble and try to explain how important you are? A little doubt can cause more doubt until you find yourself in the flesh. Leaven is like putting yeast in the dough when making bread. It looks real small but enough of it will cause the dough to rise.

Yet, God has a word of encouragement in Galatians 5:10 "I have confidence in you through the Lord, that ye will be none otherwise minded: but he that troubleth you shall bear his judgment, whosoever he be."

Get away from or do not give place to those that would question your faith in God and try to put you on a spot in an effort to pull you into the flesh and under the law.

Remember Galatians 5:16 "This I say then, walk in the Spirit, and you shall not fulfill the lust of the flesh."

Ephesians 4:17-19 "This I say therefore, and testify in the Lord, that ye henceforth walk not as other Gentiles walk, in the vanity of their mind, Having their understanding darkened, being alienated from the life of God through the ignorance that is in them, because of the blindness of their heart. Who being past feeling have given themselves over unto lasciviousness, to work all uncleanness with greediness."

Though a person is a Christian, they can still be walking in the vanity of their mind. Their understanding can still be darkened. That is not what God wants. It says, in the bible that we are to try the Spirits to see if they be of God.

See? There is a way out of this dilemma. You do not have to walk around questioning whether others around you accept you or not. You are accepted in Christ through faith and not of works. God can do more things through you as you walk in faith with Him than can be accomplished through all the works one can do.

A final reminder: Romans 8:14-21 "So that they that are in the flesh cannot please God. But ye are not in the flesh, but in the Spirit, if so be that the Spirit of God dwells in you. Now if any man have not the Spirit of Christ, he is none of his."

Why should we walk by faith? <u>First</u>, we are saved through our faith in Jesus, <u>secondly,</u> II Corinthians 5:7 says, "For we walk by faith, not by sight." <u>Finally</u>, We can conclude that there is hope for us to go on walking in faith not by law.

Romans 8:14-21 "For you have not received the spirit of bondage again to fear; but you have received the Spirit of adoption, whereby we cay, Abba, Farther." The Spirit itself beareth witness with our spirit, that we are the children of God: And if children, then heirs; heirs of God, and joint-heirs with Christ; if so be that we suffer with him that we may be also glorified together. For I reckon that the sufferings of this present time are not worthy to be compared with the glory which shall be revealed in us."

Hallelujah! We can go on because we realize that our faith in Jesus and walking by faith keeps us free from the bondage of the law. So when someone tries to question your positioning or your walk with the Lord, you can say...I have not received the spirit of bondage again to fear... that I do not live up to your expectations. My expectation is from God. As long as I walk with Him in faith then I have all the acknowledgement I need, thank you.

Even more, God wants us to know Romans 8:19 "For the earnest expectation of the creature waiteth for the manifestation of the sons of God. For the creature was made subject to vanity, not willingly; but by reason of him who hath subjected the same in hope, Because the creature itself also shall be delivered from the bondage of corruption into the glorious liberty of the children of God."

The animals are looking for the manifestation of us to walk in faith so that they can also be blessed. So come on, what do you say? Let's get out from under the bondage of the law and walk by Faith.

Unbelief

What manner of man is this that calms the wind and sea?
Why just by His hand, He plans my destiny.
Unwilling to see past what I could see,
I sit in loneliness, never feeling free.

But, when I feel His loving touch, I know, I know...
That I can trust beyond the portals of my eyes.
I see beyond the midnight skies to a place where heaven is.
I see His mercy and grace unfold beyond what I can see.

Yet, in my life there is a stillness,
That blocks my heart to sing.
The misunderstanding of His grace,
Has caused my heart to lean upon the things I see,

Unable to let the healing begin, I fall down upon my knee.
I find myself praying, lost in heartache and despair.
What has happened to my song in the night?
Why has the stillness of my soul taken flight?

A DRY AND THIRSTY LAND

Have I been to the end of my rainbow? Has darkness engulfed my soul?
When misunderstandings take the place of faith, and trust and belief,
The saddened soul takes hold and leads us down paths yet untold.
Yet, in a second, a glance of light comes streaming towards my soul.

A remembrance of His faithful love,
With yet more stories untold.
My saddened heart awakens from sleep
And I arise with healing in my wings.

Yet, repentance of my lonely soul now must be.
Shadowed in darkness, I awake as if from a dream.
My souls screams with an awakening of truth.
Where is the God of my yesterday?

How was it that I went astray?

Unbelief

Written By
Marilyn Marinelli

CHAPTER 23
Hope In The Midst of Change

Every year, around the close of October, the leaves begin to turn and the brilliancy of the trees captures our eyes to see their beauty. The acorns have been falling to the ground where we are. The squirrels are running here and there collecting them.

God uses a lot of references to the trees and the seed in the bible. Ezekiel 17:24 "And all the trees of the field shall know that I the Lord have brought down the high tree, have exalted the low tree, have dried up the green tree, and have made the dry tree to flourish: I the Lord have spoken and have done it." Is but one example. I am sure you can find many more.

"A Dry And Thirsty Land" is based on the loss in our lives and how God will be there even when we feel He is so far away. I guess the trees are a real good example of life. They bloom… their leaves change and grow again and their seeds fall to the ground to hopefully reproduce their kind.

I am seeing life just that way. People come and go in our life leaving seeds of children, hopes, dreams and so much more. Yet, we tend to think things don't change but they do.

Joel 2:12 "And rend your heart, and not your garments, and turn unto the Lord your God: for he is gracious and merciful, slow to anger, and of great kindness, and repenteth him of the evil."

Hosea 12:6 Therefore turn thou to thy God: keep mercy and judgment, and wait on thy God continually.

Joel 2:14 Who knoweth if he will return and repent, and leave a blessing behind him; even a meat offering and a drink offering unto the Lord your God?

In reference to the above scriptures, Samuel lost his child, experiencing the hurt, Samuel cried. Yet, God gave him another son, Solomon. I believe what God is showing us is that when we lay our hearts before him and not rip our garments in despair, we understand that God is gracious, merciful, doesn't get angry quickly and has a great amount of kindness. As in Hosea 12:6 above states, we must wait on God continually. If we repent, there is a blessing waiting for us.

The leaves have turned a scarlet red, orange and green and yellow. Yet, in the mist of the change of season there is hope. Hope thou in God. For in Him is life and life more abundantly than we could ever hope or think. For God's ways are higher than our ways.

Joel 22:5 "And I will restore to you the years that the locust hath eaten, the cankerworm, and the caterpillar, and the palmerworm, my great army which I sent among you."

Joel 2:36 "And you shall eat in plenty, and be satisfied, and praise the name of the Lord your God, that hath dealt wondrously with you: and my people shall never be ashamed."

Joel 2:28 "And you shall know that I am in the midst of Israel, and that I am the Lord your God, and none else: and my people shall never be ashamed."

God restores the years or times that we feel we have lost. We will have plenty and be satisfied and praise God for this. And we shall know that God is in our midst and that we will never be ashamed.

And again we are reminded Ezekiel 17:24 "And all the trees of the field shall know that I the Lord have brought down the high tree, have exalted the low tree, have dried up the green tree, and have made the dry tree to flourish: I the Lord have spoken and have done it."

If you are feeling like a dried up old tree, God will make you flourish as you wait upon Him.

Jeremiah 31:10-13 "Hear the word of the Lord, O ye nations, and declare it in the isles afar off, and say, He that scattered Israel will gather him, and keep him, as shepherd doth his flock. For the Lord hath redeemed Jacob, and ransomed him from the hand of him that was stronger than he. Therefore they shall come and sing in the height of Zion, and shall flow together to the goodness of the Lord, for wheat, and for wine, and for oil, and for the young of the flock and of the herd: and their soul shall be as a watered garden; and they shall not sorrow any more at all. Then shall the virgin rejoice in the dance, both young men and old together: for I will turn their mourning into joy, and will comfort them, and make them rejoice from their sorrow."

You may feel that God has scattered you but He will also gather you as a shepherd does with his sheep. God redeems you and takes you from the one stronger than you. You shall sing and flow in the goodness of the Lord; you soul (mind, will and emotions) shall be like a watered garden and not have sorrow anymore. It doesn't matter what age you are you will rejoice in dance, your mourning will turn into joy and you will be comforted and rejoice.

John 15:4 "Abide in me, and I in you. As the branch cannot bear fruit of itself, except ye abide in me."

John 15:5 "I am the vine, ye are the branches: He that abideth in me, and I in him, the same bringeth forth much fruit: for without me you can do nothing."

John 16:33 "These things I have spoken unto you, that in me you might have peace. In the world you shall have tribulation: but be of good cheer; I have overcome the world."

I pray that this article brings hope to your soul. That whatever circumstance you find yourself in, God can be there for you. Just call upon him and let Him help you heal and mend so that you can find yourself rejoicing once again.

Job 11:16-18 "Because thou shalt forget they misery, and remember it as waters that pass away: And thine age shall be clearer than the noonday; thou shalt shine forth, thou shalt be as the morning. And thou shalt be secure, because there is hope; yea, thou shalt dig about thee, and thou shalt take thy rest in safety."

Jeremiah 17:7 "Blessed is the man that trusts in the Lord, and whose hope the Lord is."

Shall I dare to say anymore?

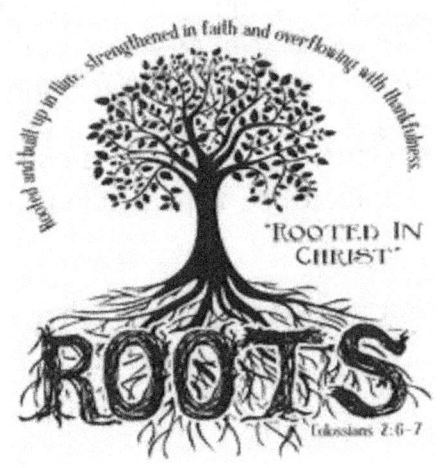

CHAPTER 24
Restoring Your Peace

Our peace, in troubled times, can some times be lost. Then fear begins to move in and rage takes over. What a crowd. Is your peace under attack? Does fear rage inside of you? No not me, I'm blessed. Why should I take a look at me, me, and me? How about all these other people and all these other circumstances that trip me up. I was happy before they all showed up.

Now come on let's face it, we all would like to blame someone else for our problems.

It's so much easier. Sure I'd rather blame anyone else but me. But guess what, they don't care or aren't even aware how they are affecting you, you, you. You're the one that is walking around with no peace inside with fear trailing behind and sure enough something stupid comes out of your mouth and rage just may raise its ugly head. So, looking at me, me, and me may be a really good idea. As we look at Me! Me! Me! Let us see what God says in His word to help us get on the right track.

In Philippians 1:4, God says, "My brethren dearly beloved and longed for, my joy and crown, stand fast in the Lord, my dearly beloved."

My, what a greeting, God loves us and longs for us. We are a joy and crown.

Philippians 4:6-8 "Rejoice in the Lord always: and again I say, rejoice. Let your moderation be known unto all men. The Lord is at hand. Be careful for nothing; but in everything by prayer and supplication with thanksgiving let your request be made known unto God. And the peace of God, which passes all understanding, shall keep your hearts and minds through Christ Jesus. Finally, brethren, whatsoever things are true, whatsoever things are honest, whatsoever things are just, whatsoever things are pure, whatsoever things are lovely, whatsoever things are of good report; if there be any virtue, and if there be any praise, think on these things.

Wow, God is telling us to be happy, how? "I don't want to be happy. I've lost my peace. I'm sitting in fear. I'm going to just blow my lid." But, God is saying to us that we first need to come to Him in prayer, letting Him know our request. Then we will receive peace... Peace from God that other people couldn't understand. Peace that you could have in your situation, because they couldn't have it without God's help. God then instructs us as to what to keep our minds on. What is true, pure, honest, lovely, of good report, if there be any virtue, or any praise, think on these things. I'm sure it does not take an o.k. God, I got it. It takes application each day, at every turn and circumstance. You want peace? Then you need to work on it. God will always help us as we apply His directions to our life.

Are you still with me? Let's go on and see what else God has to say to help us to keep our peace during troubled times.

Colossians 3:8 "But now you also put off all these, anger, wrath, malice, blasphemy, filthy communication out of your mouth."

Ouch ....

II Corinthians 5:7 **"For we walk by faith, not by sight."**

Think about that! If we walk by faith, then we see how God wants us to see the situation. If we walk by sight, we could just about lose it. Can't we?

God understands that we will have tribulation but reminds us that Jesus has overcome them all, as in John 16:33 "These things I have spoken to you, that in me you might have PEACE. In the world you shall have tribulation: but be of good cheer; I have overcome the world."

But how am I going to do this, Lord?

John 16:13 "When he, the Spirit of truth, is come, he will guide you into all truth: for he shall not speak of himself; but whatsoever he shall hear, that shall he speak: and he will show you things to come."

In other words, the Holy Spirit will guide us into all truth and show us things to come. It will be o.k. if we stay in our walk with the Lord and apply His word in our situation.

Ephesians 2:1-10 Let's us know that God understands where we have been but let's us know He is rich in mercy and love towards us. He reminds us that by His grace we are saved. <u>Very important!</u>

I Timothy 6:10 Shows us not to look towards money. Don't make our finances our god because many have gone down that road and found much sorrow.

What should we do instead? Glad you asked.

Acts 26:16-18 "But rise, and stand upon they feet: for I have appeared unto thee for this purpose, to make thee a minister and a witness both of these things which thou hast seen, and of those things in the which I will appear unto thee; Delivering thee from the people, and from the Gentiles, unto whom now I send thee, To open their eyes, and to turn them from darkness to light, and from the power of Satan unto God, that they may receive forgiveness of sins, and inheritance among them which are sanctified by faith that is in me."

God has not called His children to sit in fear, rage or a loss of peace. Rather, to stand in Him and minister to others.

II Corinthians 3:17 "Now the Lord is that Spirit: and where the Spirit of the Lord is, there is liberty (freedom)."

Isn't that what we all are looking for, freedom?

In Jeremiah 10:10-12 God let's us know who He is. He is the true God; he made the earth, by His power, wisdom and discretion. In Jeremiah 9:23-24… We are told not to glory in our wisdom, might or riches.

Isaiah 60:1-3 encourages us to arise and shine. That God's light has come and the glory of the Lord is risen upon us. Also, that His glory shall be seen on you.

You might say, but what about me? I'm still hurting right now. Psalm 140:12 says, "I know the Lord will maintain the cause of the afflicted and the right of the poor." God knows your hurts and will always, continually be there for you.

And our prayer should be like, Psalm 141:8 "But mine eyes are unto thee, O God the Lord: in thee is my trust; leave not my soul destitute." Put your eyes on God and trust Him and pray that your soul (mind, will and emotions) will not be barren or empty.

Psalm 53:5 shows us that they were in great fear, where no fear was: for God had scattered the bones of him that encamped against them. God had put them to shame, because God despised them. Sometimes we're just afraid of things that aren't even there any more. God has taken care of the situation, yet the fear of the past keep coming back to steal our peace.

But look at this scripture...Psalm 55:18 "He has delivered my soul (mind, will and emotions) in PEACE from the battle that was against me: for there were many with me."

Isn't that great! God delivers us in peace from the battles against us as we turn to Him for His help, guidance, and direction as we apply His word to our situations.

When we have understood and receive our victory, we can then say as the Psalmist in Psalm 41:11 & 12 "By this I know that thou favourest me, because mine enemy does not triumph over me. And as for me, thou upholds me in my integrity, and sets me before thy face for ever."

Therefore, our confession should be:

Micha 7: 7 & 8 "Therefore I will look unto the Lord; I will wait for the God of my salvation: my God will hear me. (Resurrection Power)...Rejoice not against me, O mine enemy: when I fall, I shall arise; when I sit in darkness, the Lord shall be a light unto me."

Praise God! We Win...

Can you do it? Yes. Will you do it? If you do, you will gain your peace back. Praise God.

Freedom

**Freedom, Freedom shouting
in my heart.**

A shout of Freedom that no one hears.
For the Freedom that I found
Is within my heart.
Placed in me from God above
To give me a brand new start.

Freedom from discouragement.
Freedom, from all fear.
Freedom from past hurts and shame.
Freedom all the year.

"A new person I have made you.
Free to be your own.
With my guiding hand,
You'll never be alone.

I'll take that old stony heart of yours
And melt it and make it new;
And give you joy and happiness
That all had said not true.

I'll turn your captivity
Right before your eyes
And give you peace of mind
I'll never, never lie.

Freedom rings within your soul
A gift from God above,
So that you can always be
Abiding in His love.

Written By
Marilyn Marinelli

CHAPTER 25
In The Fullness of Time

In the fullness of time, my heart sings, as the voice of a dove.... To bring to you my love, the pleasantries of days long past.... A renewal of springtime fragrances of long forgotten times, Lost in the memories of a saddened soul... Buried beneath a field of flowers... Longing to behold the sunlight of the day...Lost in a forbidden land of sorrows.... Beneath a willow tree, hidden from sight...Hidden in the sadness of time. When shall the sun light up your face? How shall it all come about? How long will it last?

Where do you go to be renewed from sorrows or strife, when time has cast its saddened days upon your life and hidden them beneath the sadness of time, in the realm of darkness? When will my soul rejoice again, oh Lord? When shall I feel your sunlight upon my face once again?

In the springtime of your soul (mind, will and emotions), I will uphold you in my delight. I will fill your days with wonders of my deliverance and light. Your feelings will change and newness will take hold upon your every day and I will not leave you wandering or going astray. You will feel my arms leading you along life's path. The sun will shine again. No more to wander through life's wrath.

The sadness that has buried your soul has been lifted. Now, instead of darkness, there will be happy shades of new. The springtime of your soul is blooming once again. It is full of hope, joy, peace and a new song.

Times have past for all to see, that no one can be found from the lonely times that buried you. Springtime reigns within your soul. No more to feel life as strange. The springtime of your soul blooms for all to see.

Sing on oh fair one of the land. Sing praises to my name and let everyone that hears your song remember Me, for I am the Alpha and Omega. The Beginning and the End.

"Many are the afflictions of the righteous but God delivers them from them all." Know that God will never leave you or forsake you. For this cause Christ died for you, that "No weapon formed against you shall prosper." He will raise up His saints.

God loves you. Wait, I say upon the Lord and He shall raise you up. Wait, I say upon the Lord.

CHAPTER 26
Word From The Lord To Us All

Listen to the voice of the Lord:

Jeremiah 9:23-24 "Thus saith the Lord, Let not the wise man glory in his wisdom, neither let the mighty man glory in his might, let not the rich man glory in his riches: But let him that glorieth glory in this, that he understandeth and knoweth me, that I am the Lord which exercise loving kindness, judgment, and righteousness, in the earth: for in these things I delight, saith the Lord."

Jeremiah 10:10-12 "But the Lord is the true God, he is the living God, and an everlasting king: at his wrath the earth shall tremble, and the nations shall not be able to abide his indignation."

Jeremiah 10:11-12 "Thus shall ye say unto them, The gods that have not made the heavens and the earth, even they shall perish from the earth, and from under these heavens. He hath made the earth by his power, he hath established the world by his wisdom, and hath stretched out the heavens by his discretion."

Jeremiah 10:14-16 "Every man is brutish in his knowledge: every founder is confounded by the graven image: for his molten image is falsehood, and there is no breath in them. They are vanity and the work of errors: in the time of their visitation they shall perish. The portion of Jacob is not like them: for he is the former of all things; and Israel is the rod of his inheritance: The Lord of hosts is his name."

A DRY AND THIRSTY LAND

Notice God's provisions for you this day my friend:

Isaiah 40:29 "He giveth power to the faint; and to them that have no might he increaseth strength."

Isaiah 40:31 "But they that wait upon the Lord shall renew their strength; they shall mount up with wings as eagles; they shall run, and not be weary; and they shall walk and not faint."

Isaiah 41:10 "Fear thou not; for I am with thee: be not dismayed: for I am they God: I will strengthen thee; yea, I will help thee; yea, I will up hold thee with the right hand of my righteousness."

Isaiah 41:17 "When the poor and needy seek water, and there is none, and their tongue faileth for thirst, I the Lord will hear them, I the God of Israel will not forsake them."

Isaiah 42:6 "I the Lord have called thee in righteousness, and will hold thine hand, and will keep thee, and give thee for a covenant of the people, for a light of the Gentiles;"

Isaiah 42:7-9 "To open the blind eyes, to bring out the prisoners from the prison, and them that sit in darkness out of the prison house. I am the Lord: that is my name: and my glory will I not give to another, neither my praise to graven images."

Behold the former things are come to pass....

Isaiah 42:16 "And I will bring the blind by a way that they knew not; I will lead them in paths that they have not known: I will make darkness light before them, and crooked things straight. These things will I do unto them, and not for sake them."

Isaiah 43:10 "Ye are my witnesses, saith the Lord and my servant whom I have chosen."

Isaiah 43:18 "Remember ye not the former things, neither consider the things of old."

Isaiah 43:21 "This people have I formed for myself; they shall shew forth my praise."

Isaiah 45:12-13 "I have made the earth, and created man upon it: I, even my hands, have stretched out the heavens, and all their host have I commanded. I have raised him up in righteousness, and I will direct all his ways: he shall build my city, and he shall let go my captives, not for price nor reward, saith the Lord of hosts."

Isaiah 45:20 "Assemble yourselves and come; draw near together, ye that are escaped of the nations: they have no knowledge that set up the wood of their graven image, and pray unto a god that cannot save."

Isaiah 49:16 "Behold, I have graven thee upon the palms of my hands; thy walls are continually before me."

Isaiah 53:9-10 "Break forth into joy, sing together, ye waste places of Jerusalem: for the Lord hath comforted his people, he hath redeemed Jerusalem. The Lord hath made bare his holy arm in the eyes of all the nations; and all the ends of the earth shall see the salvation of our God."

Isaiah 54:17 "No weapon that is formed against thee shall prosper; and every tongue that shall rise against thee in judgment thou shalt condemn. This is the heritage of the servants of the Lord, and their righteousness is of me, saith the Lord."

Isaiah 55:11 "So shall my word be that goeth forth out of my mouth: it shall not return unto me void, but it shall accomplish that which I please, and it shall prosper in the thing whereto I sent it."

Isaiah 58:12B "thou shall be called, the repairer of the breach, the restorer of paths to dwell in."

A DRY AND THIRSTY LAND

Isaiah 60:1-2 "Arise, shine; for thy light is come, and glory of the Lord is risen upon thee. For, behold, the darkness shall cover the earth, and gross darkness the people: but the Lord shall arise upon thee, and his glory shall be seen upon thee."

What do all of these scripture passages say to us?

- ❖ Glory in the Lord.
- ❖ God is all-powerful.
- ❖ Putting things before God is vanity and foolish.
- ❖ God gives power to us when we are weak.
- ❖ Strength comes from waiting on the Lord.
- ❖ We are not to fear life but embrace it because God is with us.
- ❖ God will not forsake us when we are in that dry and thirsty place.
- ❖ God has given us a covenant full of promise that He will keep on our behalf.
- ❖ God has promised us that He will set us, the captive, free.
- ❖ God leads the blind by a way they know not and will make our darkness light.
- ❖ No weapon formed against us can keep us away from God's love.
- ❖ We are to shine with His glory as a result of His great love for us.

CHAPTER 27
It's Time To Move On

It's time to move on. Most of us want to stay in what we think is a comfortable spot only to find out that it becomes more difficult to stay there than to move on.

Things become more apparent to us as we look deeper into the situation. When our hopes and dreams of what we wanted didn't pan out, we then have to look to God for our strength, our hopes and future. That's not too bad if you take time to think about it. God always has a better plan. He knows the beginning of all things and the end as well. He knows the times we have tried but also knows what was really going to happen. So I believe He has made provisions for each of us.

Didn't He say in His word that all things work together for good to those that love Him and are called according to His purpose (Romans 8:28)? Then what is His purpose for our lives? If we investigate more closely, we will see that His purpose is to have life and to have it more abundantly (John 10:10). What about family? What about the job I wanted? What about everything else in life? I could see each one of us pointing our finger that way when in fact God wants us to drop the finger pointing and look to Him to provide what is best for us. We don't want to be like Lot's wife. Remember her? Lot and his wife were leaving Sodom and Gomorrah and she turned back to look at what she was leaving and the destruction upon that city also destroyed her. We don't want to be there.

Are you saddened by that thought? Didn't you want what you wanted? How many times have you tried to go the way God wanted you to go and found out that it really was much better for you than your own way? You discovered that you were a lot happier than you had thought you could have been. If you had stayed in your wants and your expectations, you never would have experienced the more abundant life of John 10:10.

I guess this year we need to stop holding on to the things and people we think we need. They only cause us heartache and tears. We need to let God take control so we can find our times and life in Him.

"Many are the afflictions of the righteous but God delivers them from them all." God will always shine light on our situation so that we can understand that we do not need to stay there anymore, but to move on with Him and His plans for our life. Sometimes our emotions scream inside us to stay in a particular situation but we must move on in order to have the more abundant life God has promised us.

I pray that this will be the greatest time you have ever had in walking with the Lord as He leads you on to a more abundant life.

Conclusion

I would be foolish to say that the times of walking through the desert were easy or that it took just a few days. However, I would encourage you to not let go and if you do, get right back into the loving presence of God.

As you can tell through my darkened, dry and thirsty walk, the Lord was at my side. God said to me, as the rain fell against the windshield of my car and tears streamed down my face, with no one else around nor could they understand the pain I was in, "The raindrops on your window are my angels crying for you today." It was really important to know that God cared so much for me. I know He will be there for you as you seek Him in your life.

How do we get through tough times?

- ❖ By trusting in the Lord.
- ❖ By having faith that He will be there for you.
- ❖ By repenting and forgiving others.
- ❖ By confessing the promises of God.
- ❖ By standing on the Word of God.
- ❖ By not falling under the expectations of others.
- ❖ By listening for and obeying the voice of the Lord in the circumstance.
- ❖ By not giving any place to the devil.
- ❖ By praising the Lord in the circumstance, not for what is happening, but rather for His awesome power and willingness to be there with you and lead you to victory.

My Prayer

God you know my heart and all the lies and falsehoods that live within my soul. I want to do your will and minister for you –yet this snare of deception; I believe seems to take hold of me. Help – Jesus – clear the path that we may dwell and be blessed and be a blessing.

Deception

The deception lies within your soul,
Based on hurts of long ago.
Sitting on what life should bring,
Keeping you bound and covered with sin.

As you sit beside the brook,
Know what is and stop and look,
And see what plans I have for thee.
Surely they will come to be.

They are based on the lost and found.
They are based on thoughts all around.
Some are good and some are bad.
Some filled with fear of what you had.

Time flees by and you will know,
What truth is within your soul.
No more to hinder, no more to fear,
A new course in time, holding nothing near.

For all the leaves have shed their brilliancy,
Leaving you wandering and wondering where to be.
Stop, look and listen to the many sounds,
Look they're all on solid ground.

The winds have blown, so stop and see
What happened to the tree?
The devil cast his hurtful song,
But, with me you belong.

MARILYN MARINELLI

Stop and listen to the whistling of the trees,
The hurts, the fears of all the leaves.
Come sit and take my hand
And walk with me through the land.

Stop and look all around
Are their leaves left on the ground?
Saddened hearts and woeful cries,
Linger on until they die.

Shine on; shine on amidst the pain,
No more to walk on leaves filled with rain.
For truth will shine within your days,
No more to look to other's ways.

Look up, His peace restored,
Within your brokenness,
There is so much more.
For peace I give and then restore.

Shine on oh fair one of the night,
Don't forget who shined the light.
Stand up; stand up for all to see
That light shines from me.

Do not fret or even fear,
For I hold you very dear.
Place your feet on solid ground,
And free the others as they are found.

Shine on; shine on, within the night.
Make your plea for all that's right.
Be of good courage and do not fear.
The time of testing is so very clear.

Stand within this test of time,
Forever shine, always be mine.
Keep the peace and stand tall.
Don't look to those that fall.

A DRY AND THIRSTY LAND

For many trees will shed their light,
Of glimmering hope, for what is right.
Don't stand within these shadowed walls,
To listen to their beckoning call.

For their leaves will take a turn of color
And leave others with stormy weather.
Shine on; shine on for all to see
For you are planted as God's seed.

Shine on,
stand the test of time,
Forever my love
You are always mine.

Written By
Marilyn Marinelli

A Final Thought

Micah 7:5 "Trust you not in a friend, put not your confidence in a guide."

Job 11:16-20 "Because thou shall forget thy misery, and remember it as waters that pass away: And thine age shall be clearer than the noonday; thou shalt shine forth, thou shalt be as the morning. And thou shalt be secure because there is hope; yea, thou shalt dig about thee, and thou shalt take thy rest in safety. Also thou shalt lie down, and none shall make thee afraid; yea, many shall make suit unto thee. But the eyes of the wicked shall fail, and they shall not escape, and their hope shall be as the giving up of the ghost.

www.ingramcontent.com/pod-product-compliance
Lightning Source LLC
Chambersburg PA
CBHW050440010526
44118CB00013B/1607